THE LAST GOAL HE EVER SCORED

THE LAST GOAL HE EVER SCORED

THE LIFE AND LEGEND OF BILL BARILKO

RONNIE SHUKER

sh.
SUTHERLAND HOUSE

TORONTO, 2026

Sutherland House
416 Moore Ave., Suite 304
Toronto, ON M4G 1C9

First edition, October 2026

If you are interested in inviting one of our authors to a live event or media appearance, please contact sranasinghe@sutherlandhousebooks.com and visit our website at sutherlandhousebooks.com for more information about our authors and their schedules.

We acknowledge the support of the Government of Canada.

Manufactured in Canada
Cover designed by Lena Yang

Cover image courtesy of Hockey Hall of Fame, Michael Burns Sr.
Book composed by Karl Hunt

Library and Archives Canada Cataloguing in Publication
Title: The last goal he ever scored : the life and legend of Bill Barilko / Ronnie Shuker.
Names: Shuker, Ronnie, author
Description: Includes bibliographical references.
Identifiers: Canadiana (print) 20260239437 | Canadiana (ebook) 20260239445 | ISBN 9781997701606 (hardcover) | ISBN 9781997701699 (EPUB)
Subjects: LCSH: Barilko, Bill, 1927-1951. | LCSH: Hockey players—Canada—Biography. | LCGFT: Biographies.
Classification: LCC GV848.5.B37 S58 2026 | DDC 796.962092—dc23

ISBN 978-1-997701-60-6
eBook 978-1-997701-69-9

In honor of Bill Barilko,

and for those who carry his story forward

Contents

Sudden Death

Imagine for a minute you're William Barilko. You come from a poor family in a Northern Ontario mining town, and you're just twenty-four years old. Tonight, you're going to play in a Stanley Cup Final game against the great Montreal Canadiens. And you don't know this yet, but it's going to be you that they hoist up onto their battered shoulders. You. You're going to kiss the girl and drink from the Cup as an entire nation celebrates you. Until the bony hand of fate plucks you from the sky.
—Oliver "Brokentooth" Solaro, *Blue Line*

SOME NHL TEAMS TEACH arrogance, others teach indifference. The Toronto Maple Leafs teach longing. Being a Maple Leafs fan means carrying around emotions that defy intellectual defense. Embarrassment braids permanently together with devotion. Rational people would've abandoned their inheritance generations ago, but loyalty to the Leafs is unconditional and lies beyond the bounds of reason. It is cultural birthright disguised as sports allegiance.

For those of us born into the cult of the blue and white, we grow up learning surnames the way Catholics learn saints: Jackson, Conacher, Clancy, Apps, Kennedy, Horton, Armstrong, Keon, Bower, Sittler, Salming, Clark, Gilmour, Sundin. These are the legends of Leafs history, the finest players the franchise has ever iced. Yet none of them ever authored a moment as big and beautiful as a young defenseman from Timmins did, here in the city's old secular shrine at what was once the most famous intersection in the country.

As I step off the streetcar and cross the street, the building on the northwest corner pulls me inside like a wayward sheep from the flock. It isn't nostalgia that's brought me here. How could it? The moment happened long before I was born, long before my parents had met and even conceived the idea, much less the being, of me. Sure, I once skated within its walls as a Timbit-sized seven-year-old in the Timmy Tyke Tournament in the early 1980s, and I once watched Toronto's boys in blue beat those cold-blooded, red-deviled Soviets of Moscow Dynamo in an exhibition game as a fourteen-year-old later that same decade. But what I know of the greatest goal scored in Leafs history comes from the memories of others, passed down in books, in songs, in ceremonies.

I pass through the sliding glass doors of the old building's new entrance, negotiating my way around people with bags, baskets, backpacks, and carts of groceries. On my right, above the escalators connecting to the mezzanine, hang several dozen blue seats arrayed in a large Leafs logo. Where crowds once surged in to see the Leafs chase Stanley Cups, people now drift through stands of bread and fruit and between freezers of frozen pizzas and ice cream, pausing in front of photographs and plaques that whisper of a past faded but not erased. Beneath bright grocery lights and within the bones of the old building, the past has been folded into the daily rhythm of the present, so that buying groceries becomes, almost without noticing, a short stroll through the history of the city's old cathedral of hockey.

Maple Leaf Gardens.

This place always felt like hallowed ground to me, even glimpsed on the screen of a bulky old floor-model cathode-ray-tube television set while parked on my parents' living room chesterfield as a kid or, later, seen through the first flat-panel TVs lounging on the faded couches of my dingy college and university apartments. It still does now through the 4K OLED screen from the comfort of my California-made, fire retardant–free sofa in the living room of my suburban home north of Toronto, nearly thirty years after the Leafs moved from the city's former civic center at Church and Carlton to their current home down by Bay Street and the Gardiner Expressway. The prospect of an urban revitalization project turning the glorious Gardens into a grotesque grocery store initially felt like the city had turned its back on its team, discarding the past while trying to monetize the memories. But the soul of the place is still here. The oversized signage advertising the CANTEEN, BAKERY, DELI, and GRILL honors the past grandeur of the old building, while the store's merchandising and promotional material have copied the industrial stencil font once used in the old concrete stairwells. Outside, the art deco brick facade, preserved marquee, and domed roof all remain, as do the windows, light fixtures, and ghostly concrete eastern wall inside, exposed rebar and all.

I find aisle twenty-five and walk past a large pillar in the middle. On the floor at the end of the aisle, flanked by cans of Spam, tuna, and corned beef on one side and spaghetti, lasagna, and various other pastas on the other, lies a blank blue maple leaf inside a white circle trimmed in red. In the middle of the maple leaf is a white dot.

Center ice. It all started here.

Behind me, a plaque on the pillar describes the history of this spot in the kind of braggadocio that could only ring true in Canada:

> *The place upon which you stand served as Canada's centre stage for nearly seven decades.*

Then begins a list of the Gardens' greatest moments: its opening on November 12, 1931; the Leafs' historic comeback in the 1942 Stanley Cup Final after losing the first three games to the Detroit Red Wings; their three-peat in 1949 to become the NHL's first dynasty; another three-peat in 1964; followed by the franchise's final Stanley Cup in 1967.

They are all triumphs in the long-standing tradition of the Leafs. But the greatest of them all came in the middle of those moments, seventy-five years ago today, on April 21, 1951:

> *In the final game of the 1951 final, Bill Barilko scored the overtime game-winning goal against the Montreal Canadiens in the last game he would ever play.*

Bill Barilko. His spirit is still here. If these walls could talk, they would tell a tale so fantastic as to be almost Faustian. But even though Barilko played like a raging hellfire on the ice, he was fed far too much hockey humble pie to have ever done a deal with the devil. Equal parts mythic and mysterious, triumphant and tragic, his is a real-life story so surreal and ghostly that it reads like it was scripted. That Hollywood played a pivotal part in it is only fitting.

I don't know exactly when the story took hold of me, but I know the reasons why. It was inevitable, really. A player from my home province (Ontario), sharing the game I grew up playing (hockey), from the team

I grew up watching (Toronto Maple Leafs), whose story was resurrected by the band I grew up listening to (The Tragically Hip) was destined to captivate me at some point in my life. It's been called Canada's Amelia Earhart story, or its Buddy Holly story. Yet while the comparisons are apt, they are unfortunate. All too often, in all too Canadian fashion, we search for an American analogue to a Canadian story, as if somehow seeking permission from our nearest neighbor to tell our own stories to ourselves in our own home and then sheepishly searching for the confidence to share them with the world. Leafs fans should know the story the best, but most never look beyond Barilko's banner hanging in the rafters of Scotiabank Arena, and most Canadians never dive deeper than the song that brought his story back to life. We've all heard his name, many of us have even sung it, but most of us don't know the story. We don't know how it happened, why it happened, and, especially, *where* it happened.

I know I didn't. For thirty years, I'd belted out the verses about Barilko in The Tragically Hip's "Fifty Mission Cap" without knowing who the lyrics were actually about. It wasn't until 2022, when I first ventured to the site of the plane crash that killed him, that I began to understand the significance of his story: a blue-collar boy born into a blue-collar immigrant Ukrainian family in a blue-collar mining town in Northern Ontario who worked and willed his way from the mini Maple Leaf Gardens replica in Timmins all the way up to its architectural archetype in Toronto, via the beaches and beauty of Hollywood, and scored the greatest goal in Leafs lore, only to perish in a mysterious plane crash while on a fishing trip four months later, not to be found for eleven years.

The Barilko story isn't just a Leafs story, nor only an NHL story, or a hockey story, not even a Canadian story. It is a universal story of the human condition, of a life lived to its fullest in the shortness of time. We all experience triumph and tragedy, every one of us. Barilko just experienced them at their highest pitch. All these years later, his story is still being written: through the grocery store that honors and preserves his memories and moments; through the writers who've written books and the bands who've created songs about him; through the people who removed the wreckage from the Northern Ontario forest where fate pulled the plane from the sky; through the die-hard Leafs fan who has the remains of the wreckage tastefully displayed in his basement; through those who erected a privately funded billboard to honor his story in his hometown; through the northern adventurers who feel compelled to try to visit the crash site overland through the impenetrable muskeg of the Hudson Plain; and through all the fans who make pilgrimages to Barilko's gravesite, wear Barilko jerseys, and carry on the legend. The Barilko story is now their story.

I circle back toward the entrance of the store, passing by a handful of people sitting at long tables in front of a big screen showing a soccer game. Each table is themed with photos of Gardens gatherings: political events, basketball games and figure skating competitions, concerts, boxing and wrestling matches, and more sports. Farthest from the screen is the hockey table, where I find a photo of Barilko being carried on the shoulders of his teammates after scoring his overtime goal. I pull up a chair, slide my laptop out of my backpack, slip on my headphones, and pop open a video synced to the radio call seventy-five years ago.

Gray and grainy film footage of the play moves across the screen, the Leafs on the left and the Canadiens on the right. The pace is faster than I expect. Perhaps it's just been sped up, but it could also be the rush of adrenaline that would inevitably come with playing in overtime of game five in the 1951 Stanley Cup Final.

I watch and listen as Foster Hewitt, from his perch aloft in Maple Leaf Gardens, narrates the torrid pace of overtime. Players' surnames spill out of his mouth with heart-pounding urgency as the Leafs take it to the Canadiens: Leafs forwards Harry Watson and Howie Meeker, Canadiens goaltender Gerry McNeil.

> *Watson comes back fast at center ice . . . Skating down the left wing . . . Into the corner . . . Shoots and hits the side of the net . . .*

Hewitt's high-pitched nasal voice builds and builds as the Leafs attack the Canadiens' net. A broken play raises his pitch ever further. Hewitt is calling it faster and faster, but he can hardly keep pace with the play.

> *Here it's right in front to Meeker . . . Meeker went by the net . . . Centered out in front . . . McNeil fell . . . In front again . . . Watson shoots . . .*

The puck bounces off the net, into the slot, off a stick, off a skate, and then slides slowly out into the face-off circle to the right of the Canadiens' net. But Hewitt never sees what's coming. For out of nowhere, Barilko suddenly appears. In a moment that's since echoed throughout Leafs history, NHL history, hockey history, Canadian history, Barilko flies into the screen as he makes a desperate dive for the puck and backhands it over the flailing McNeil. Utterly absorbed in his frantic call of the frenetic play, Hewitt isn't even able to table the possibility for his three million listeners (nearly a quarter of Canada's population at the time). The moment arrives before we even know the name of the man who authored it. Hewitt screams in his iconic call at 2:53 of overtime:

> *He shoots, he scores!*

And then:

> *Barilko! . . . Barilko has won the Stanley Cup for the Leafs! . . . Barilko shoots it into the net while McNeil was left all by himself . . . The Toronto Maple Leafs are the world champions.*

I close my laptop, take off my headphones, and lean back in my chair. Seventy-five years to the day it happened, this is the closest I'll ever come to experiencing the moment. I try imagining what the city must have felt like back then, before disappointment became our civic inheritance: radios encircled in tiny postwar kitchens as overtime unfolded, families leaping from their living room chairs when the puck crossed the line, strangers yelling from apartment windows in rapture of another Stanley Cup. But try as I might, I'll never know what it felt like to be there, to be one of the 14,577 fans who witnessed the greatest goal in franchise history, or one of the millions listening across the country. I cannot go back to when it happened. I cannot go back in time.

But I *can* go back in space, to the places where the story, and everything associated with it, happened. In honor of Barilko, I've planned a pilgrimage that will reconstruct his career path, retrace his fatal flight path, and then follow the legacy he's left behind. That is why I am here, in a grocery store on the northwest corner of Church and Carlton, where the legend was realized; why I'm going to Timmins, where Barilko was born and raised; to Hollywood, where he began his uncharted ascent to Toronto, via Pittsburgh and Buffalo; to a pair of university arenas in Toronto that bookended his five seasons as a Leaf; to the Leafs' current arena, where the spirit of Barilko is on full display; to a law office in the city's east end whose space Barilko and his brother used to set up a business for life outside of hockey; to a run-down industrial stretch of the city where an unlikely piece of street art pays tribute to Barilko's shining moment; to the lake where the plane carrying Barilko departed on a fishing trip and never returned; to the two towns on the doomed return flight home along the east coast of James Bay where he was last seen alive; to the dense muskeg of the Hudson Plain where the plane crashed and Barilko disappeared; to the basement in a Toronto suburb where the remains of the wreckage rest in memory of the fallen Leaf; to his final resting place, where Leafs fans continue to pay their respects; to a concert of a band from his hometown still singing his name; to the Hockey Hall of Fame, where his name isn't included among the inducted but should be; and to all the unlikely points in between, where fans and pilgrims continue his legacy, long after his life, which burned so bright for too short a time, was tragically extinguished.

No one knew it that night in Maple Leaf Gardens, least of all Barilko, but the biggest moment of his career, of his life, would be his last goal, his last game, his last Stanley Cup.

"It was a long time coming," Barilko said after the game. "It was something I've dreamed about doing all my life."

Four months later, Bill Barilko was gone.

The Northern Spirit

Bill was all alone on defense with two men coming at him. Instead of trying to outwit them, he walked into the guy on the right and started a battle. I liked his moxie and decided that if he ever learned to skate he'd make the grade.

—Johnny Mitchell, Toronto Maple Leafs scout

NORTHERN ONTARIO IS THE Labrador of Central Canada. Rugged, rocky, untamed, it is a vast frontier of ancient lakes, formidable forests, harsh winters, and hardy humans. A province within a province, it's defined more by where people don't live than where they do. Distant from its capital and too often misunderstood by its government, it makes up nearly ninety percent of Ontario's land area yet just six percent of its population. Underneath the armor of the Canadian Shield, its abundant natural resources have given birth to single-industry towns where self-reliance is a necessity for survival.

Opinions vary on where Southern Ontario ends and Northern Ontario begins. Most draw a long line from Sault Ste. Marie in the west, through to

Sudbury and North Bay, and ending just above Ottawa in the east. Others push this imaginary border down to Northern Ontario's most southern administrative boundary, which includes Parry Sound, the birthplace of Bobby Orr. All I know is that if I keep driving up from Toronto, I'll increasingly feel the steady pull of the North.

After visiting Maple Leaf Gardens, I leave my home at the northern edge of the city and head up Highway 11. It is spring, but winter is fighting a holding action as I head north. Stubborn patches of snow run alongside the road, and birches beam bright white against the dark of the black spruce. The acrid air of the city begins to give way to the smell of damp earth, thawing grass, and the faint iron scent of waters waking beneath their ice. The highway winds through fields and forests still undecided between white and green as I make my way through towns like Huntsville, North Bay, Temagami, and Temiskaming Shores. The farther the road stretches, the quieter the country becomes as the towns thin out and gas stations stand solitary along the roadside. When I reach the town of Matheson, I turn onto Highway 101 and follow it west, into the city that built Bill Barilko.

Welcoming me to Timmins, from his billboard across the road from Porcupine Lake, is the city's four-time Stanley Cup champion, dressed in his white Toronto Maple Leafs sweater, his right fist pumped in the air and a victorious smile across his face after scoring his overtime goal in the 1951 final.

Before Toronto, before Barilko's overtime overture, there was Timmins. Long before he became a Maple Leaf, Barilko was just another kid chasing big-league dreams amid dwindling daylight on frozen ponds and frigid rinks in this part of Northern Ontario. Timmins of the time wasn't a place that coddled its kids. It was a mining town, toughened by bitter cold, hard work, and isolation, a place that produced people who learned quickly how to endure and children who had to grow up early. Barilko's boyhood, shaped by small-town values, a community that revolved around work, and a culture that centered on hockey, laid the foundation for the man who would one day define a dynasty in Toronto.

By the time William Barilko was born on March 25, 1927, Timmins was barely a generation old, carved out of the wilderness following the Porcupine Gold Rush in the early part of the twentieth century. The boy's Ukrainian parents, Steve Barilko, who arrived before World War I, and Feodosia "Faye" Karpinchuk, who arrived after it, were part of a wave of Eastern European immigrants who came to Northern Ontario lured by the promise of streets paved with gold but settled for steady work in a working-class hub defined by mines, mills, and rail lines. Steve found work as a cook in mining camps, while Faye took care of the home and raised their three children: Alex, Bill, and Anne. Like many Timmins households, the Barilko family lived modestly. Indulgences like movies, restaurants, soda, and ice cream were rare, and sharing space, food, and responsibility was a fact of existence. The rhythm of life mirrored the shifts underground and followed the seasons above it.

Back then, Timmins was the hub of a sprawling area called the Porcupine that included the wards of Schumacher, South Porcupine, and Porcupine. Timmins absorbed them all in 1973. In the 1930s and '40s, Timmins, and its surrounding settlements, was a loud and gritty place, boasting large French-Canadian, Italian, Croatian, Finnish, Polish, Yugoslavian, Romanian, and Ukrainian communities. The place was prosperous and full of hope. The clank of machinery, the smell of smoke in the air, the scarred landscape of slag heaps and open pits represented an economic oasis in the midst of the Great Depression. Men worked dangerous jobs deep below the surface. Women kept households running with discipline and ingenuity. Kids learned independence early.

Sports were an approved outlet for what little space life left for recreation. As a boy, Barilko loved hunting, fishing, swimming, and softball. But in a town defined by winter, summer was little more than the interlude between hockey seasons. In Timmins, hockey wasn't just a game. It was part of the cycle of life, seamless and fluid. For much of the year, outdoor rinks glowed against the dark northern sky, filled with the crack and thwack of sticks and the cackle of kids dreaming of NHL fame.

Barilko didn't fall in love with the game in a single instant. It seeped into him slowly, inevitably, osmotically, through the impromptu games played on any one of the frozen ponds and outdoor rinks in and around town, the pickup road hockey games played in alleyways, the floor hockey bouts with his siblings using a marble and ruler in the kitchen, and Saturday nights spent parked in front of the family radio listening to Foster Hewitt call games from Maple Leaf Gardens as Barilko imagined himself as a Leaf lining up alongside the great Charlie Conacher.

Barilko learned to play the game the way most kids in Northern Ontario did in the 1930s. There were no specialized coaches, development programs, or hockey academies. Kids played on cleared ponds, flooded lots, and makeshift rinks scraped together by volunteers. Skates were hand-me-downs (Barilko got his from his father's boss). Sticks were taped and retaped until they snapped. Protective equipment was minimal, often nonexistent. If Barilko got hurt, he shook it off. If he fell behind, he worked harder.

Where Barilko learned to play is what shaped how he played. Conditions on Timmins' outdoor rinks were rarely perfect. Pucks bounced, snow drifted in, and ruts ran through the ice. Fingers numbed and toes froze, but spirits were always high. Those conditions rewarded resilience more than elegance and perseverance more than gracefulness, and enforced the importance of improvisation. Even after he'd made it all the way to the big-time in Toronto and started winning the Stanley Cup with remarkable regularity, Barilko never forgot where it all began for him and how hard he'd worked to get there.

"Ten years ago, I couldn't skate and they made me play goal," Barilko recalled as a twenty-year-old with the Leafs. "One year in the nets was enough. I about froze to death."

After that short-lived season as a goalie, Barilko promised himself he would never return to the crease, unless it was to cross-check an unwelcome opponent out of it. There was just one problem. The boy couldn't skate to save himself. He was a bowlegged ankle-burner who chopped at the ice like he was trying to fell timber with his skates. It would take him months to figure out the way of the blade, an art form he would eventually learn but never master.

"I was on the ice morning, noon, and night learning to skate," Barilko said. "By the next fall, I was good enough to play defense with my brother."

That Barilko would find his home on the blueline was inevitable. Half of it was physical, the other half was instinct. He was bigger and stronger than most of his peers, and he craved contact, whether making a hit or taking one. He savored the moments when an opponent would come down his side of the ice, knowing both of them were going feel the effects of the inevitable collision.

"It was fun bouncing guys and being bounced," Barilko said. "I was determined to stay on defense if I had to skate eighteen hours a day."

I continue into Timmins until I come to McIntyre Arena, just south of the Porcupine Miners Memorial and the McIntyre Mine Headframe. In Timmins, mining and hockey never stray far from one another. I can feel the old mining settlement that the city once was and still partly remains. Hard-rock miners, Ukrainian families, smoke from the mines staining the sky. Men with blackened fingernails and burdened shoulders skating on frozen ponds after shifts underground, or drowning their disdain every payday for the lives they lived below. Barilko was born of this world. He wasn't polished; he wasn't manufactured. He belonged to the rough northern spine of Ontario that built itself on the backs of men and women who earned everything and expected nothing.

A scaled-down replica of Maple Leaf Gardens, the arena opened in 1938. Its construction was financed by local businessman and mining entrepreneur J. P. Bickell, who'd worked with Leafs president Conn Smythe to get the Gardens built seven years earlier. "The Mac" gave the town a gathering point and an identity beyond the mines. Proud of the players it produced, the town rallied around its teams. Local leagues for company teams, school teams, almost any kind of team, drew strong crowds. Rivalries were intense, especially against other nearby northern communities, where pride was on the line as much as the score. Here, hockey mattered. It offered something resembling hope to kids like Barilko, who grew up watching older players being treated as local heroes. They weren't famous. They simply represented the town well, their play reflecting the ruggedness of the land and the hardiness of the people.

I walk inside the doors of the adjoining McIntyre Coffee Shop, an old-school diner and a muster point for many of the community's inhabitants. The place feels less like a restaurant and more like an enduring corner of northern life, the kind of place where the morning settles in slowly with the steam of coffee and the murmur of friendly voices. The original stools wait at the counter for returning patrons, while battered, chrome-framed chairs gather around simple wooden tables crowned with condiments. At the back of the restaurant are several blue vinyl booths, worn smooth by decades of conversations. I claim one of them and sit down to eat.

Along the walls, framed photographs of local players past watch over patrons, everyone from hometown heroes Frank Mahovlich and Steve

Sullivan to lesser lights like Don Lever and John Kovich. Interestingly, most of the framed jerseys mixed in among the photos are of former NHLers who aren't even from Timmins, players like Jonathan Cheechoo (Moose Factory), Joe Thornton (London), Darren McCarty (Burnaby), and Brian Savage (Sudbury). At the counter, stainless steel gleams beneath the warm lights, while coffee cups clink and the television flickers above. At a large round table, a cluster of regulars lean in close, trading opinions and predictions that hang heavy in the air like the scent of greasy bacon and buttered toast. I smile at the thought that this place has quietly witnessed countless ordinary mornings like this one, filled with hockey talk and mine gossip.

I finish my meal, a lumberjack's breakfast in a miner's diner, and then walk through the restaurant's internal entrance to the adjoining rink, past the Lil' Orbits mini donuts stand and a display case exhibiting photos of the famed Flying Fathers ("Praying and Playing"). Over the far blue line, behind the scoreboard above center ice, hangs a sixteen-foot-long banner of Barilko.

Timmins hockey values effort above all else. Players are expected to finish their checks, play through pain, and respect the game and their teammates. These unwritten rules, as much in place today as they were in the 1940s, shaped Barilko more than any drill ever did. By his mid-teens, it was clear he'd worked his way to being better than most kids his age in town, largely by virtue of being both bigger and meaner. From high school and air cadet teams, he graduated to more seasoned and competitive juvenile, junior, and senior clubs: the Timmins Canadiens, the Hollinger Greenshirts, and (briefly) the Porcupine Combines, where he played with his older brother, Alex. The leagues weren't glamorous, but they were challenging. World War II loomed over everything in a town that contributed heavily to the war effort, both in soldiers and resources.

With so many older players away, it also provided a proving ground for someone like Barilko, too young to serve overseas. Never a good student, he'd even dropped out for a year to drive a truck for a local mine. The war years accelerated his hockey development during his most formative years. He was no longer just a local prospect. Forged in one of the harshest hockey environments in the country, he was a young defenseman on the rise, with a mix of size and hostility and a reputation for hard hitting that bruised bodies on the ice and turned heads in the stands. Scouts began to take notice, particularly those keeping an eye on Northern Ontario.

When Johnny Mitchell went up to Timmins in the fall of 1944 to scout players, he came away thinking about an aggressive young man on defense, a one-man wrecking crew who skated like he was running on ice. Impressed with the kid's mojo, if not his skating, Mitchell made a mental note to check on the player later in the hockey season.

When Mitchell followed up on Barilko in the spring of 1945, this time in Toronto, where Barilko was playing with the Combines during a showcase at Maple Leaf Gardens, he found the same punishing player but one whose skating, though still lacking anything resembling grace, had become a strength not a weakness. Mitchell's endorsement of the blond-haired bodychecking blueliner from up north eventually reached the highest rung of the Leafs' organizational ladder.

"There's the one I want," Smythe told Mitchell when he saw Barilko for himself.

From there, Barilko's destiny was determined. Timmins had done its job. He was now ready for the pros. His hometown had hardened him, challenged him, shaped his instincts. The town's winters had strengthened his legs, its rinks had heightened his awareness, its people had taught him humility and resolve. It produced a player who didn't need to talk about toughness because he lived it. A player who understood that hockey, like life in the mines, rewarded those who showed up ready to work. When Barilko left Northern Ontario, he carried Timmins with him in every sense.

I leave the arena, drive through the heart of town, and navigate a set of side streets until I come to Timmins Memorial Cemetery, opposite a blueberry patch where the Barilkos used to pick berries as a family. Two rows deep into Section E of the Historic Protestant Sites section, I find two side-by-side headstones marked BARILKO. One is for Steve and Faye Barilko. The other is for their son Bill.

In 2018, former NHL player Bill Riley was watching a segment on *Hockey Night in Canada* when a glimpse of Barilko's grave stopped him cold. The headstone was covered in a crust of moss and hardened dirt, its inscription nearly illegible.

Riley had never set foot in Timmins, but he grew up worshipping the Leafs and was a huge fan of The Tragically Hip. The image of the neglected stone troubled him. Had Timmins been closer, he would've climbed into his vehicle and driven there himself, all the way from his home in Nova Scotia if he had to. Instead, he picked up the phone and called his daughter, Tracey, who'd moved to Timmins the year before.

Tracey could hear the emotion in her father's voice. As an ex-NHLer, having played for the Washington Capitals and Winnipeg Jets in the 1970s, he believed deeply in the brotherhood of hockey players, that those who'd worn an NHL crest belonged to something greater than themselves.

Gathering cleaning supplies, rubber gloves, and a stiff-bristled brush, Tracey made her way to the cemetery. Armed with a map, she wandered the quiet grounds until she found Barilko's resting place. Then she knelt and began to work.

As she scrubbed away the layers of moss and grime, a sense of pride rose within her. Not only for the task itself, but for what it meant to her father. The cemetery was still except for the scrape of the brush against stone. Before long, she found herself speaking softly to Barilko, as though he were listening.

When his headstone was finally clean and the carved letters stood clear once more, she adorned it with a few flowers and then turned her attention to his parents' stone beside his and cleaned theirs too, leaving the family's names visible again beneath the northern sky.

Standing before Barilko's headstone, I'm struck by the beautiful craftsmanship. Below his name and years he lived are the four years he was a Stanley Cup champion: 1947, 1948, 1949, and 1951. At the bottom is his end: DIED ACCIDENTALLY AUG. 26, 1951—BURIED JUNE 15, 1962. All of it is flanked by engravings of maple leaves, hockey sticks, and pucks. Trinkets from fans, including a loonie, line the stone's base.

At the top, beneath his surname in all caps, is a head-and-shoulders photo of a beaming Barilko adorned in a Leafs sweater, long before jerseys came along. His blue eyes are colorless in the black-and-white image, but his blond hair is meticulously coiffed. If you look close enough, you might even see a hint of a Hollywood smile.

Hollywood Hockey

Hollywood has a terrific prospect in seventeen-year-old Bill Barilko, a rugged defenseman who wades into the biggest opponents without blinking an eye. You'll hear from him in years to come.
—Braven Dyer, *Los Angeles Times*

AFTER TIMMINS SHIPPED HIM south, and before Toronto beckoned him back north, Bill Barilko called Hollywood home. Inside the now-vanished shell of the Pan-Pacific Auditorium, his dreams of playing professional hockey soared as high as the four towers of the auditorium's facade, the finlike spires that resembled the rakish bow of some streamlined ocean liner pointed forever toward the future. The building burned down in 1989, flames devouring the wooden structure until only its skeletal towers remained against the dawn. I watched the footage before I flew here. The auditorium collapsed sorrowfully, as if exhausted by years of abandonment and decrepitude.

Replaced by Pan Pacific Park, the old grounds have been repurposed and stitched into the city's flood control infrastructure. It is now ordinary in the way unconsecrated places become sacred when someone comes searching for a now nonexistent piece of the past. I find what I'm looking for at the entrance to the park's recreation center, where a single forty-five-foot tower pays homage to the old auditorium. A ghost of its old four green-and-white fins, their nautical curves and aerodynamic ribs have been copied for this melancholy monument.

I walk toward it. Up close, the replica retains something theatrical of a time when crowds arrived in fedoras and evening dresses to see a young Canadian defenseman bruising bodies in the California heat. Yet nothing remains of the spectacle that once drew sellout crowds here, just the everyday human tide that now moves across the acreage. Everything here is temporary, even the myths.

From Los Angeles, I head southeast toward Anaheim, navigating an endless braid of traffic to Disneyland Resort, where music drifts through artificial streets scented with caramel and machine oil. Here, the Pan-Pacific Auditorium has been polished into nostalgia. Deep inside the grounds stands another reproduction of the arena's old facade, this one fully transformed into the four-finned entrance to the Disney California Adventure's old gateway district. Here, too, I sense the strange ache of continuity. An architectural fossil from a demolished arena has been reborn inside the dream-factory of Southern California. Families wander underneath the towers without knowing that a teenager from Timmins had once played hockey behind their original incarnation.

I imagine Barilko, stepping outside the arena after a game, the uncertainty of minor-league life hanging over him like the city's haze. He was just another young player from Canada carrying his skates into the California dark, chasing a dream like everyone else in the city.

It seems so much the stuff of destiny that even the mythology feels prefigured. A story that would later be told and retold in song didn't truly begin to take shape until Barilko stepped onto the ice at an arena in Los Angeles known more for its architecture and its audience than for its sports teams. Here, far from winter's wrath in Northern Ontario, hidden away from the hopeful but hesitant eyes of the Toronto Maple Leafs executives who'd sent him to Southern California, Barilko began to learn how to harness the undirected energy of his game under the curious eyes of a largely uninitiated crowd thirsty for novelty and hungry for impact. In that sunlit American chapter of an otherwise Canadian tale, Barilko chiseled away at the mass of raw material he'd been trying to sculpt into form upon the ponds and rinks of Timmins until, though still naive and untested, he had the makings of a professional hockey player, prepared for the colder, harder, heavier road ahead in Toronto.

That foundation was laid near the intersection of West Beverly Boulevard and Fairfax Avenue at the Pan-Pacific Auditorium. Inside, its modest interior, which could sit nearly six thousand screaming fans, was Southern California's muster point for major indoor events, everything from political rallies, exhibitions, circuses, conventions, concerts, and car shows, to basketball, tennis, wrestling, and hockey.

This became Barilko's home when he landed in Los Angeles in the fall of 1945 in the waning weeks of the war. When he first stepped off the plane into the warm, salt-tinged air, it must have felt like he'd wandered off the edge of the only map he'd ever known. He paused for a moment, suitcase in hand, hockey gear waiting for him in baggage claim, a Northern Ontario boy suddenly surrounded by boulevards and ocean air, feeling both the thrill and the loneliness of being so far from all he'd known, like a man who'd skated out past the blue line and realized the rink had grown impossibly large beneath his feet. In Timmins, the world had been iron-gray skies, hard snow, and the factory-like routine of a mining town where winter seemed to settle into the bones of everything. In Hollywood, palm trees lifted their fronds against a bright sky and the streets hummed with a restless energy, as if the whole place had been built as a kind of stage.

The crowds that would cheer Barilko on to Toronto were everything unlike the hardcore hockey fans of home. Long before the likes of Tom Hanks, John Candy, Will Ferrell, and Snoop Dogg would frequent the NHL's Los Angeles Kings, the Hollywood Wolves of the Pacific Coast Hockey League would draw in celebrities like Cary Grant, Bing Crosby, and Frank Sinatra, as well as actress Vera-Ellen, who had major roles in *On the Town* and *White Christmas* and became such a promotional fixture with the team that she was eventually made its official mascot. In Hollywood, hockey was looked upon more as entertainment than sport, and the players were expected to put on a show. Barilko didn't disappoint. With his physical playing style, coupled with a fierce determination to make Los Angeles his springboard to Toronto, he became an instant fan favorite. It was the perfect combination: Barilko brought the grit, Hollywood delivered the glamor.

He arrived ahead of the 1945–46 season, wide-eyed and wondrous, after the Maple Leafs shipped him there out of training camp. Barilko joined a Wolves club that'd finished toward the bottom in the inaugural season of the PCHL, a West Coast circuit born out of a merger between the Southern California Hockey League and the Northwest International Hockey League. At eighteen years old, he was the youngest player on a team that featured a mixture of wily veterans looking to get back to the NHL and greenhorn junior players just hoping to get there for the first time. It was an all-Canadian team in the unassuming hockey hotbed of Hollywood that played a Canadian brand of hockey in a league made up almost entirely of Canadian players.

The PCHL wasn't just born out of novelty. World War II had made it something of a necessity. With players heading overseas to serve the war effort, the NHL had been drained of talent, rerouting the pipelines of pro hockey. Leagues were reshuffled, teams remade, and rosters reshaped, sending players to corners of the continent where they otherwise would've never plied their trade. Officially, the PCHL was an amateur league, but salaries were disguised as living expenses, and the pay was on par or even higher than the minor-pro leagues out east. One of two teams in Los Angeles, with others in nearby San Diego, San Francisco, and Oakland, and four more in the Pacific Northwest, the Wolves were the PCHL's most flamboyant franchise. They were competitive, ambitious, and hungry for legitimacy. They wanted to prove that hockey in Hollywood wasn't some sideshow. Games were promoted aggressively, sometimes with show-business flair. Fans packed the Pan-Pacific Auditorium, and home games were even broadcast on local television in Los Angeles, long before it ever became the norm in the NHL. The Wolves set league records for attendance and gate receipts. They were such a success that Hollywood later applied for an expansion franchise with the NHL. Barilko played his part, captured in a promotional photograph in the Wolves' star-speckled jersey, jamming to a stop at the side of an empty net, kicking up a spray of knee-high snow, eyes the size of saucers, ready to pot a loose puck.

Fans, many of them new to the game, responded viscerally to speed and contact. A clean, open-ice hit received the same roar as a goal, and so Barilko, despite scoring only fifteen goals over his time with the Wolves, often earned the most and loudest cheers. With more than one hundred penalty minutes in his first season, he led the team and was tied for third in the league. That off the ice, he was polite, courteous, mild-mannered only helped boost his popularity with local fans.

That summer before he joined the Wolves, scouts from the Leafs had liked what they'd seen out of Barilko in training camp with the American Hockey League's Pittsburgh Hornets, the organization's top affiliate, where Johnny Mitchell was general manager. As did Leafs president Conn Smythe, a decorated veteran of both world wars. Still a growing teenager, Barilko wasn't the most towering presence on defense, but he played with a mix of raw physicality and reckless abandon alongside an unshakable desire to step into traffic that struck fear into oncoming forwards, except for those who possessed the speed and skill to swing wide and outskate his attempts to bang them permanently into the boards. As the Wolves' coaches and executives quickly found out, there were far too many of them. They would have work to do with their youngest player.

Barilko, you see, was far from fleet of foot when he arrived in Hollywood. Every stride chopped at the ice, like the hacking thrusts of a speed skater at the start of a race. In reverse, he looked more like a floundering gazelle in retreat than a wily wolf leading on its prey. At training camp with the Hornets, oncoming forwards had frequently turned him into a turnstile, blowing by him with ease off the rush. If Barilko ever hoped to make it from a Wolf to a Hornet, much less a Leaf, he would have to learn to skate all over again, just as he'd done in Timmins. Only this time, backward.

Whatever talent he had, it never got noticed, nor exploited. It was Barilko's sheer hard work that had caught the eyes of Leafs scouts. But to catch the attention of the Leafs' front office, Smythe in particular, he would have to work even harder. And so, he did. Hour after hour, day after day, practice after practice, Barilko willed his way into becoming a powerful pro-level, if not entirely graceful, backward skater.

Running the show for the Wolves in Hollywood was coach Bob Gracie, who'd played parts of nine seasons in the NHL, winning the Stanley Cup twice, including once with the Leafs. Under Gracie's tutelage,

Barilko learned not only to skate backward, but to cultivate an instinct for making the thousands of instantaneous decisions hockey demands. The playcalling of football, the pitch selection of baseball, the half-court offense of basketball, they all afford their players time to decide, to plan, to predict. Not hockey. To succeed in the game, instruction must become instinct. Under Gracie's watchful eye and barked orders, Barilko molded his all-out, unstructured, hair-on-fire playing style into something that could survive in the more disciplined and ordered NHL. He learned when to jump into the play and when to back off, when to apply pressure and when to release it, when to take a risk and when to play it safe. That instinct didn't come fully formed in Toronto. They rehearsed, over and over and over again. Backstage in Hollywood, where the expectations were lower but the demands were very real, was the perfect place to learn.

Still, the Wolves understood that they couldn't keep losing. Success as a team would only come from winning, and Barilko was central to that push. He anchored a defense corps through stretches when offense came and went. He didn't chase praise, he chased results, blocking shots, clearing the crease, breaking the puck out. But it was his board-shaking bodychecks that would become his career calling card and would draw the biggest cheers.

During Barilko's first season as a pro, Mitchell flew out to check on his progress. He watched as Barilko got clocked in a line brawl that left him with a cut over one eye. As Mitchell went down to the first aid room to check on the young defenseman, he could hear a voice yelling all the way down the hall.

"Get that doctor in here!" Barilko screamed. "I want to get out there and even with the guy who got me."

Mitchell was sold.

Even though it was founded in the cushy confines of California, the PCHL was anything but soft hockey. The further down a minor-pro league was from the top of hockey's pyramid, the rougher and tougher it often was and the more unpredictable it could be. Ice conditions were never uniform, officiating was inconsistent, and games often devolved into lawlessness. Barilko was in his element. Fights, blocked shots, and errant sticks left him bloodied, stitched, and scarred but never beaten.

Coaches and teammates witnessed firsthand how Barilko reshaped his game over his first season with the Wolves, while local newspapers documented his metamorphosis. Beat reporters and columnists who began the season saying he lacked "steadiness and experience" would describe him as "ever-improving" by midseason and "one of the better defensemen in the league" by the end of it. The Wolves rode their roughhousing teenage defenseman all the way to a spot in the league final, losing to the original incarnation of the Vancouver Canucks. By then, it was clear to everyone that something special was brewing in Southern California.

Back home in Timmins, in the summer of 1946, Barilko spent the offseason skating and training at McIntyre Arena, and swimming and fishing when he wasn't on the ice. It was a summer of great loss for Barilko, with the sudden death of his father, Steve. He would never see his son play in the NHL.

As the 1946–47 season drew near, rookie camp with the Leafs and then another training camp with the Hornets only convinced the organization that Barilko, though much improved, still wasn't quite ready for the NHL. So, back he went to Hollywood for more seasoning. His second stint featured yet more of the turnover and transition that are the hallmarks of minor-league hockey. The Wolves brought in former NHL player and league MVP Tommy "Cowboy" Anderson, pairing him with the team's now nineteen-year-old defenseman.

In his second season with the Wolves, Barilko continued to use his body as a battering ram, much to the delight of the Hollywood faithful. A favorite target of his, for both chirps and hipchecks, was the player–coach of the rival Los Angeles Monarchs, "Big" John Polich. Whenever the Wolves and the Monarchs met, always at the Pan-Pacific Auditorium, which they shared as their home arena, fans were guaranteed to see Barilko and Polich square accounts. Even though Polich was eleven years older, three inches taller, and nearly twenty pounds heavier, Barilko never backed down from a fight, not from him nor anyone else. No one, not even big brother Alex, who was chasing the same dream as a member of the rival Oakland Oaks, was safe from the Wolves' thumper. In one game, the brothers, neither recognizing the other, were battling hard for the puck in the corner during a blowout win for the Wolves. The two turned around instinctively to drop the gloves and start throwing bombs. Only a last-minute flash of recognition saved the brothers from a chiding by their mother back home in Timmins.

With both brothers in Southern California, Alex and Bill crossed paths regularly in their respective pursuits of the NHL. After one game between the Wolves and Oaks, the two sent their mother a message in what remains the only known recording of Barilko's voice. The closeness between the brothers is clear. Even when they played against each other, they still "played together."

"The sun is shining bright down here," Bill begins. "I guess it's starting to snow up there. Well, Mom, Alex will be here for a couple of days with me, and we're really going to have a good time."

"We sure are," Alex says. "Last night, we played together, and they beat us two–one, Mom. Bill knocked me down a couple of times, but I got back at him."

"Oh, now, listen here. None of us got hurt, though."

"No, nobody gets hurt when we play together, Mom. Don't worry about that."

The Wolves soared to the top of the PCHL during the regular season and would've likely made another run at the league championship had their teenaged tour de force stuck around. But Barilko's steadily improving play and skating, helped along by Anderson's mentoring, hadn't gone unnoticed in Toronto.

In early February 1947, just as the season was about to enter its home stretch, the Wolves were getting ready for a Saturday night home game when a call came in from Toronto. It was Smythe. With the Leafs in the midst of a five-game winless skid, and the team's defense corps drained by injuries, Smythe had called down in search of reinforcements. He wanted to know more about the player they were calling "Billy the Kid." Asked for his assessment, Anderson had plenty of praise for his young defense partner.

"He's green," Anderson said. "But he's a big boy, not scared of anything, and eager to learn."

For Smythe, who once said, "If you can't lick 'em in the alley, you can't beat 'em on the ice," that was all he needed to hear. Barilko was his kind of player, one whose confidence bordered on cockiness. By the time he came face-to-face with Smythe for the first time, Barilko would boldly tell the man who could cut him off the roster just as easily as he would cut his checks, "Your troubles are over."

Barilko played that night but left the ice during the third period when the announcer told the crowd that one of their own was getting the call-up. He was pulled from the game to a standing ovation from the fans and to handshakes and congratulations from his teammates. By midnight, he was on a plane to Pittsburgh, where he was expecting to join the Hornets, the natural next step up in his pursuit of the NHL. But Barilko would never see anything more of Steeltown than its airport.

Billy the Kid

I'll never forget Barilko's first game. Down in Montreal, and Elmer Lach come down center. Just as he passed to Maurice Richard, Barilko belted him, and Lach bounced into Richard and they both went into the boards. He was banging them all night. We lost the game 8–2, but we won a lot after that because there wasn't a forward in the league that wanted any part of Bill.
—Conn Smythe, Toronto Maple Leafs president

PITTSBURGH APPEARS BENEATH CLOUD cover, all bridges and rivers and blackened hillsides. After my flight from Los Angeles, I spend the night at a hotel downtown overlooking the Monongahela River. When Bill Barilko arrived here decades earlier in a wrinkled suit, carrying everything he owned in one bag, he was unaware that the Maple Leafs had summoned him directly to Toronto. After leaving the Hollywood Wolves to a standing ovation, and then changing out of his equipment, Barilko had taken a red-eye here, expecting to join the Maple Leafs' top farm team, the Pittsburgh Hornets of the American Hockey League. It wasn't until he touched down and deplaned that the team's general manager, Johnny Mitchell, told him he was going all the way up to the Leafs. In the middle of a two-day journey, stitched together through winter delays and exhausted improvisations, he was only halfway between the Pacific dream he'd left behind and the hard reality ahead at the northern edge of Lake Ontario.

From Pittsburgh, I board an overnight train northeastward. The farther I travel, the more the landscape resembles the world Barilko would've seen slip past the window. I watch from my sleeping berth as the train rattles through freight yards, industrial towns, and slumbering fields. Garbage collects along sidings and riverbanks as steel towns drift by and smoke rises from factories into low skies. By the time I reach Buffalo, the station smelling faintly of diesel fuel and wet wool, morning has settled. I take a bus across the border into Niagara, carrying my bag through customs under pale fluorescent lights, while mist drifts invisibly from the falls.

When Barilko arrived here by train from Pittsburgh, he did so in the midst of a blazing midwinter blizzard. He checked in with the team and was told to take a taxi to Toronto. Practice was at ten o'clock that morning. Desperate not to miss his first taste of life as a Leaf, Barilko hailed a cab and told the driver to lead-foot the long ride to Toronto. Such urgency belonged to his era, when careers could disappear overnight and every opportunity seemed temporary.

From Niagara, I rent a car and follow the Queen Elizabeth Way to Toronto. At Highway 427, I join the city's tortuous traffic then cut across the Gardiner Expressway and on into downtown as impatient commuters weave in and out of traffic, motorcycles sneak in between the rows of frustrated drivers cursing under their breaths, and trucks roar past like migrating animals. Beyond all the office towers and condominiums and decades of change, it all started here for Barilko. It wasn't Hollywood, with its palms and fantasy architecture, nor Pittsburgh or Buffalo or Niagara. It was Toronto, it was the Leafs, the city and team he'd spent so many Saturday nights dreaming of.

I think of the replicated towers in California that I've left behind, those green-and-white fins preserved after the building where Barilko had burnished himself into a professional hockey player burned to the ground. It was architecture surviving as memory, then memory carrying on as pilgrimage, a trip made in honor of a dead defenseman still traveling endlessly between cities because people like me refuse to let the story ever end.

From a long-demolished auditorium, life had led Barilko here, by plane, train, and taxi, to the city that would claim him forever. He hadn't slept in more than two days, but shut-eye wouldn't come easily. Daydreams had filled his head as the cabbie hightailed it to Toronto. Far away in Southern California, still glowing in the rising Pacific morning, stood the towers of the Pan-Pacific Auditorium, forever welcoming crowds that continue to fill the site long after it was razed. Now in Toronto, as snow fell heavily through the streetlights, the fantasy that'd filled his imagination as a kid with thoughts of wearing the Maple Leaf crest on his chest had arrived with urgency.

The cab entered downtown mere minutes before Barilko had to hit the ice. The streets were still wet with salt and slush, as the cabbie carried on to Varsity Arena, where the Leafs were practicing temporarily. It is here, not Maple Leaf Gardens, where Barilko first became a Leaf.

Varsity Arena lingers in modern-day Toronto like an old archival photograph, its cold air still alive with the same scrape of skates and crack of sticks that have echoed throughout its walls in the one hundred years since it was built. Completed in 1926, the arena has endured, adapted, and been renovated in careful increments but resisted transformation.

Even demolition, which looked possible when the University of Toronto and the Leafs engaged in discussions and designs in the early 2000s about replacing the aging arena. The talks got far enough along to produce designs featuring two underground rinks, one of which the Leafs would've made their practice facility. In the end, it came to nothing.

Today, the arena doesn't announce itself boldly. Instead, it hides in plain sight, folded into the larger Varsity Centre on the campus of the University of Toronto. From Bloor Street, after dropping off my rental car, the way in feels almost secretive as I walk through the ticket office and along an outdoor corridor beneath the grandstand of Varsity Stadium. Only here, off to the right, does the arena reveal itself, its redbrick face so understated that I would've missed it entirely had I not been looking for it. Inside, the rink has retained its original wooden seats, some seating two and others just one, worn smooth by generations, with a few modern seats intruding here and there.

In its heyday, the arena bore witness to a game and a city still carving out its hockey identity through the Toronto Varsity Blues, a program, founded in 1891, that predates most of the structures around it and carries a lineage that stretches beyond the campus to the first days of the Leafs. It was with the Blues that Conn Smythe, father of the Leafs, found his foothold in the game as a player and captain while studying civil engineering at the University of Toronto and, later, as coach after graduating. It was also from where he "borrowed" the Blues' sweater design when Smythe, backed by Timmins businessman J. P. Bickell, salvaged the financially floundering green-and-white Toronto St. Patricks and rebranded them the blue-and-white Toronto Maple Leafs in 1927, the year Barilko was born.

With a touring ice show having taken over Maple Leaf Gardens for a week, Smythe watched intently from his creaky wooden seat in the rink's otherwise empty seating bowl as Barilko stepped onto the ice at Varsity Arena with the rest of the Leafs. His arrival was unceremonious. There was no prospect hype, no red-carpet rollout for the team's newest defenseman. With three rookie rear guards already on the roster, in Gus Mortson, Garth Boesch, and Jimmy Thomson, and five rookies in total, the Leafs were flush with first-year players and would ice three more, in addition to Barilko, over the rest of the season. There was only Smythe's cool, measuring stare, coach Hap Day's unequivocal instructions, and the unspoken understanding among the players that wearing the blue and white was regarded as a privilege, an honor that had to be earned every shift and could be taken away the next. The Leafs were already a proud and successful franchise, on their way to becoming a national institution, and they didn't indulge newcomers easily. Barilko wasn't brought in to dazzle. He was expected only to survive long enough in Toronto to be sent back to Hollywood.

To management, Barilko was little more than a body subbing for a banged up and bandaged blueline. To teammates, he was just a temporary replacement. But Barilko brought something with him from Hollywood. He had a smile, a swagger, and a penchant for showmanship that would shine bright under the white-hot spotlight of Toronto. He had an air of inevitability, an expectation of permanence, and an edge that Smythe supremely valued, Day dearly wanted, and the team sorely needed.

Barilko's time in Hollywood had honed his unpolished skills, but it hadn't softened the essence of the player. He was still the same belligerent, broad-shouldered bruiser, only bigger, having shot up three inches and adding twenty pounds of muscle. At five-foot-eleven and 184 pounds, he immediately became one of the bigger players in the league at the time. He was raw physical force, and force mattered mightily in the NHL of the 1940s.

Exhausted from thirty-six hours of travel, Barilko jumped onto the ice for his first practice with the team. Day, who spent thirteen seasons in Toronto as a player and won the Leafs' first Stanley Cup in 1932, wasted no time prepping his young reinforcement. A former defenseman himself, the coach spent fifteen minutes with Barilko going over some individual drills, then threw him into the mix with the rest of the team, pairing Barilko with Wally Stanowski on defense for line drills.

"He made a few mistakes, drifted too wide for rushes, but otherwise was fine," Day told reporters afterward.

After practice, Toronto's horde of media, as voracious and all-consuming then as it is today, thronged to Barilko's stall to check out the team's newest and youngest player. Winter's fury may have been raging outside, but it was clear that Barilko still had his head in the clouds.

"Boy, the sun is shining," he told them as he changed out of his gear and into his street clothes.

The 1946–47 Leafs were a mix of veteran savvy and youthful energy. On the one hand were thirtysomethings Syl Apps, the team's gentlemanly captain, and Turk Broda, its brick wall in goal. On the other were Ted Kennedy, a budding superstar at just twenty-one years old, and twenty-three-year-old rookie Howie Meeker, the team's second-highest goal scorer. Barilko would fit right in on defense with fellow greenhorns Mortson and Thomson, two tough defensemen for whom penalty minutes were simply the penance they had to pay to exact a pound of flesh from opposing forwards. With only four players over thirty years old and more than half the roster under twenty-four, the Leafs were the youngest team in the NHL. In the not-yet-twenty Barilko, they'd swept up another cannonball of energy, making them even younger and hungrier. And the Leafs' youngest player had no plans on returning to sunny Southern California.

"Don't worry about the Kid," he told his new teammates after practice. "They're not chasing the Kid back to Hollywood. I like this big-time stuff."

It didn't get any bigger than a game at the Forum in Montreal against the first-place Canadiens and the league's best goal scorer, Maurice Richard. Two days and two more practices later, Barilko boarded a train to Montreal, where he would introduce himself to the hockey world and put the Canadiens on notice that they were going to face rough times ahead.

Every player, whether a one-game wonder or a future Hockey Hall of Famer, remembers their first NHL game. When Barilko first stepped onto the ice at the Forum, on February 6, 1947, it was the realization of a boyhood dream. The morning had arrived like it does for every rookie about to make his NHL debut. Barilko awoke before the dawn, the way children do on Christmas morning. For a moment, he laid still, knowing that nothing about his life would be ordinary again. There was an expectant calm about the day. At the arena, he savored every movement leading up to puck-drop, from the slow tying of his skates to the smell of leather lingering in the dressing room and the pregame banter between players. The crest on his chest felt heavy, as if it carried every sacrifice that'd brought him there. His thoughts flickered through years of pond hockey and early morning skates, each memory rising like a breath in subzero air. No one was watching him then. Now some fifteen thousand were about to see him take NHL ice for the first time. True to form, they would boo Barilko mercilessly at every opportunity.

Somewhere beyond the concrete walls, the crowd began to gather, their voices a distant murmur that rose with each passing minute as the game grew closer. Excitement and fear knotted together in his chest, indistinguishable as he stepped onto the ice for warm-ups and the arena lights bloomed above him like a sudden sunrise. It wasn't just a game. It was the moment when a lifetime of hoping finally became real.

Until the drop of the puck pulled Barilko, or at least the rest of the Leafs, back to reality.

That night in Montreal, the scuffling Leafs were no match for the skilled and stingy Canadiens. By game's end, the home team had sent the visitors packing back to Toronto, battered and beaten after an 8–2 trouncing. Barilko had taken his lumps, but he'd dished them out, too. He was pretty much the only Leaf who showed up to play that night, taking runs at Richard, Elmer Lach, and Butch Bouchard and hitting just about every other Canadien in sight. His showing earned him praise from the team's otherwise eviscerating scribes as the Leafs' lone bright spot in what was an otherwise embarrassing and demoralizing loss.

On the return trip to Toronto, Barilko lost himself in more daydreams. As a boy growing up in Northern Ontario, he'd spent winter evenings leaning close to the radio, listening to Foster Hewitt's voice float out across the airwaves from Maple Leaf Gardens. In those moments, the Gardens felt impossibly far away, almost like another world. Yet now the train back to Toronto was carrying him toward it. The boy who'd once imagined the arena through the static crackle of a broadcast would soon see the lights for himself, feel the cold air of the ice against his face, and pull a blue-and-white sweater over his shoulders, stepping at last into the place where his imagination had been skating for years.

In Montreal, Barilko's first NHL game had taken place in one of hockey's great temples, the fabled Forum. Now here he was in Toronto, two nights later, sitting in the Leafs' dressing room at the grand old Gardens, about to make his home debut in the city's cathedral of hockey.

Like so much of Barilko's story, the night seemed scripted, as if he'd written it himself in Hollywood and simply acted it out right there on the ice in the Gardens. Late in the third period of a what would be 5–2 win over the Boston Bruins, Barilko scored the final goal of the game, taking a pass from Meeker and rifling it past Bruins goalie Frank Brimsek. The moment the puck slipped off his stick and found the net, he felt the world rush inward all at once. The crowd inside the Gardens rose like a breaking wave, hats and voices tumbling together in a thunder that seemed to shake the rafters. Only seconds earlier, he'd been another young defenseman in the blue and white, playing against the proud black and gold of the Bruins. Now, he stood in that brief, glowing pause after a goal, aware in a quiet corner of his mind that he'd just scrawled his first line into the long, hard story of the NHL. Somewhere beyond the boards, thousands were shouting, but inside him there was a strange calm, a stillness that comes after the puck hits the back of the net and the whole rink waits half a heartbeat before the noise begins.

But it wasn't Barilko's first NHL goal that got him onto the sports pages and into the hearts and minds of Leafs fans across Canada. Fittingly, newspapers ran a photo of Milt Schmidt, the Bruins' superstar, draped over Barilko's left shoulder, skate blades arched toward the ceiling, mouth agape, and eyes full of fear as he flew ass over teakettle, knowing he was about to engage in a first-class face-plant with the ice, courtesy of a Barilko hipcheck. All that was shown of Barilko was his big barrel behind and part of his number 21.

One week later, Barilko took a pair of penalties as he and the rest of the Leafs chased Richard around the ice while the Rocket single-handedly earned the Canadiens a 4–4 tie with a hat trick. The next day, after an overnight train to New York, the Leafs were bombed 6–2 by the lowly Rangers. Again, Barilko left his mark upon his opponents, scoring his second goal, a right corner top-shelf special, then dumping diminutive Grant Warwick with another hipcheck and backing it up by pummeling the much smaller man when he sought vengeance for the insult of an insolent nineteen-year-old rookie taking aim at a six-year veteran. Just four games into his NHL career, Barilko's venomous "snake hips," as his lethal hipchecks were already being labeled in the press, had become his ticket to staying in the NHL.

"I'm going to make hockey my career," Barilko said after the game. "So I'm sure going to give everything I have to stay up here with the Leafs. It's a different, tougher game than any I've ever played, but getting a couple of goals to start sure helps the old confidence."

Game after game, win or lose, Barilko would leave the ice a yard sale of opposition players who'd dared test his side of the ice. He was never starstruck. Richard, Schmidt, Roy Conacher, it didn't matter. When it came to bodychecking, Barilko believed wholeheartedly in equal opportunity. Everyone received the same ungrateful greeting from the burly young defenseman. In the ninth game of his budding NHL career, a 3–3 tie with the Detroit Red Wings, Barilko hit Sid Abel so hard that the Red Wings' centerman had to use the boards for support to make it back to the bench. He felled two other Wings, Pete Horeck and Doug McCaig, like he was knocking down bowling pins. Barilko's physical style of play was wearing out opposition forwards, and his equipment.

"I'm going to have to put some extra padding on my left hip," Barilko said. "That's the one that's been hitting them, and it's getting awful sore."

In the NHL of the 1940s, players were expected to play through injuries. The schedule was a six-month grind fueled by rivalry and packed with intensity. In the era of the Original Six, every game felt like a reckoning. It was the same teams, game after game, over and over. There was no escaping a rival. Montreal, Detroit, Boston, Chicago, New York, they were all out to take down Toronto. For a newcomer like Barilko, there were no easy games, no easing into the league with the playoffs just around the corner. If he made a mistake against the Canadiens on a Saturday night, he would see the same players again soon enough, ready to exploit a rookie defenseman still in his teens whose tenure in Toronto was as tenuous as the playoff spot the Leafs were chasing.

With so many injured defensemen out of the lineup, the Leafs had no choice but to throw Barilko into the fire. He made his fair share of mistakes, as Tommy Anderson had warned Smythe he would. With the faster pace, his reads were sometimes a split-second late, and he often chased a hit when playing the puck would've kept him out of the penalty box. But Barilko was a quick and eager study. He learned how to force a winger wide instead of into the middle of the ice. He understood that a simple, unspectacular but efficient play would earn more praise from Smythe, faith from Day, and trust from teammates than a game-breaking goal. Yet when the game tilted toward chaos, when a battle broke out in the corner, when a winger tried to cut through the middle with his head down, when opposition ruffians tried to take advantage of the Leafs' legion of skill players, Barilko came alive. He hit like a man who believed in the virtue of contact and defended his fellow Leafs like they were his blood brothers. Teammates noticed, opponents recoiled.

Offensively, Barilko carried no eye-popping statistics, at least to today's eyes. After four points in his first five games, the Leafs might've mused that they'd discovered an offensive gem hidden in the roughhousing body of a defenseman and then deployed him accordingly. They should have, but didn't, and never would, even though Barilko would go on to become one of the NHL's best goal-scoring defensemen of his playing days. He played the game with a defenseman's thunder and a forward's hunger, with an instinct for offense and a calculation for collision on defense. But he was still young, impulsive, subject to risk, and he'd brought a little too much of Hollywood with him to Toronto. In the NHL of the 1940s, defensemen, especially teenaged ones, weren't supposed to leave their posts. They were to play it safe and leave the scoring to the forwards. But Barilko liked to jump into the rush, to pinch in from the point, to be part of the play. This drew his coaches' ire on more than one occasion.

What truly defined Barilko's first season in Toronto, though, was how easily he fit into the team's culture. With Smythe at the top, playing for the Leafs was about discipline and duty. Instructions were to be taken as orders, and orders were to be followed with military precision. Barilko did just that, putting in his work and then returning to his apartment down the street from Maple Leaf Gardens when done. In a dressing room full of strong personalities, Barilko's easygoing off-ice nature, so at odds with his intense on-ice demeanor, fit in seamlessly.

As the regular season wound down, Barilko was no longer simply a rookie fighting to stave off demotion. He'd become part of the regular rotation. But the playoffs were a different dimension. Every play carried consequences, and any mistake might end the season. If Smythe and Day were hoping to see what they really had in Barilko, they were about to find out.

The Leafs entered the postseason with confidence, and for good reason. As the highest-scoring and most penalized team in the league, they possessed a beautiful and brutal mix of skill and savagery. They had scoring, depth, goaltending, youth, and an edge that could wear teams down in the meat grinder of the playoffs, especially with Barilko in the fold.

With the Leafs firmly ensconced in second place, an opening round matchup loomed against the Wings. With a rookie Gordie Howe and a twenty-one-year-old Ted Lindsay, these were not yet the big bad Wings that would bring the Stanley Cup home to Detroit four times in the early 1950s. So, aside from the second game, in which Barilko was on the ice for half a dozen goals against in a 9–1 drubbing, the Leafs dispatched the Wings with relative ease in five games to set up a showdown with the first-place Canadiens, who'd put away the Bruins just as quickly in their semifinal matchup.

Toronto–Montreal was already the league's defining rivalry. Any game against the Canadiens was an event to mark on the calendar and carried its own electricity. The matchups crackled with hostility and pride. But 1947 was the first time the archrivals had met in the Stanley Cup Final since the league's inaugural season in 1917–18, when the Maple Leafs were known as the Toronto Arenas. Playing in his first NHL postseason, Barilko found himself in an atmosphere where every hit hurt and every whistle was taken as an opportunity to get under the opponent's skin. He responded the only way he knew how. With bad intentions and that big left hip.

As the defending champions, the Canadiens played the part of the favorites, putting the Leafs on notice that they were in for a fight with a decisive and chippy 6–0 shutout win in the first game. From there on out, however, the Canadiens played right into the Leafs' plans as the series devolved into chaos. It put a smile on Smythe's face, a smirk on Day's, and brought a gleam into Barilko's eye.

Barilko was a force in the second game, scrawling his name all over the scoresheet with two assists and a pair of penalties. Just like in his first NHL game, Barilko took direct aim at Richard, unafraid of being burned by the Rocket. This started a series-long feud that would throw Richard off his game, aid in getting him suspended for slashes on teammates Vic Lynn and Bill Ezinicki, and help hold him scoreless in all but one other game in the series, as the Leafs went on to win the final in six games.

Not three months earlier, Barilko had been holding down the blueline at the Pan-Pacific Auditorium in Hollywood, hoping for nothing more than a flight to Pittsburgh and a call-up to the Hornets. Now, here he was, in the epicenter of Toronto, holding hockey's holy grail in the middle of Maple Leaf Gardens on a Saturday night in front of 14,546 fans who began the evening chanting "We want the Cup!" and ended it getting exactly what they wanted.

In the hundred-plus years of their existence, the Leafs have seen legend after legend go their entire career without ever even reaching the Stanley Cup Final, much less winning it. Darryl Sittler, Börje Salming, Wendel Clark, Mats Sundin, none of them ever tasted that glory. Just twenty-nine games into his NHL career, and only a few weeks after turning twenty years old, Barilko had already become a Stanley Cup champion.

"I realized a life's ambition that night," Barilko recalled months later. "I never dreamed I'd make it so soon, but I knew in my heart someday I'd help the Leafs win a Stanley Cup."

What made Barilko's first season so remarkable was the route he took to get there. From Timmins to Hollywood to Pittsburgh to Buffalo and, finally, to Toronto, he'd taken a road never traveled. Fans would've called it fate. He would've called it hard work. Barilko had earned the right to be in Toronto, however circuitous his route there had been. No one carried him, no one coddled him, no one demanded any more or less than what he could deliver. He'd dished out pain, absorbed punishment, learned systems, and earned trust. For that, he rewarded the Leafs with heavy hitting, sturdy defense, timely offense, and a willingness to battle beyond Smythe's profusion of military metaphors. The Leafs didn't coddle the kid and didn't hand him ice time easily. Smythe wasn't one for sentimentality, and what mattered to Day was performance, not hype. Barilko's responsibilities and ice time had increased in step with how he played, not because of any promise of untapped potential he possessed.

In purely statistical terms, Barilko's first, albeit abbreviated, NHL season doesn't leap off the page: three goals and ten assists for thirteen points. But players are remembered in moments, even if history judges them by numbers. Some meet the moment, but most draw back from it. Barilko seized his as soon as it came his way.

As summer arrived, Barilko went back to his offseason life in Timmins, carrying with him the knowledge that he'd already lived a moment most players never reach. His first season had given him validation, confidence, and a good shot at a permanent place on the Leafs. He had more stories to tell, and far more ears eager to listen. He also had more to train for, because he now had more to lose than ever.

Bashin' Bill

Barilko may not yet be the best of his kind, but he will assuredly fight a rattlesnake for the puck, spot it the first two bites.
—Andy Lytle, *Toronto Daily Star*

I FIND A SPOT IN the stands. Seated across the ice, a group of students talk animatedly but softly, while a young couple canoodles in a corner below the press box. Beneath the sheen of fresh ice and modern lines, there lingers a haunting echo of roaring crowds, a sense that the past hasn't vanished but simply settled deeper into the bones of the building, rising up like a sacrificial offering into the sacred sky of girders above the rink.

I rest my arms on the seats on either side of me and then look up. The old cathedral ceiling of the city's once secular shrine. Refurbished rather than replaced, it is a memory that refuses to fade, its steel ribs arching in solemn symmetry, bearing the echoes of crowds cheering and the ghosts of champions once lionized in the rafters. It was never just a roof. It was a steel-boned firmament, dimly lit and sanctified, where banners swayed in an ecclesiastical glow, like stained glass in a winter church. That high-end supermarket next door is a little disorienting for any fan of Toronto Maple Leafs history, but here feels a little more right. When the building was reborn as Toronto Metropolitan University's Mattamy Athletic Centre, and the rink renamed Mattamy Home Ice, the ceiling remained, preserved with a kind of reverence, watching over the ice below, just as it did when the Maple Leafs called this their home. Under this high, hallowed vault, the past clings stubbornly to the girders, as if time itself has been asked not to leave but only to make room, so that every game played beneath it now carries a quiet undertone of history, like a hymn still humming long after the choir has gone.

It is here that Bill Barilko began his first full season as a Leaf in the fall of 1947. Only a year earlier, he'd been playing at the Pan-Pacific Auditorium in Los Angeles in front of six thousand fans largely uninitiated to the game. Now, here he was, a full-fledged member of the team he grew up cheering for, playing to a full house of hardcore hockey fans beneath the domed roof and cathedral ceiling from where Foster Hewitt called games that spilled out of the radio in the Barilko family's home. He was no longer a curiosity, no longer simply the collision kid from Timmins who'd arrived in Toronto with miner's shoulders, a country grin, and a thirst for impact. He'd spent his first season with the Leafs on probation, living in fear of being sent back to Hollywood, but had survived his initial test in the NHL, won a Stanley Cup, and learned what it meant to play defense for the Leafs.

Now, he had to prove that it wasn't a fluke.

The 1947–48 season would become the year Barilko stopped being a promising young defenseman and became a full-blooded NHL force, the year his name stopped being spoken with a question mark attached to it. In a league with only six teams, under the merciless scrutiny of the Toronto media, Barilko didn't just hold his ground. He staked his claim to it.

The Leafs entered the season as defending Stanley Cup champions. It sounded grand, but no team had gone two in a row since the Detroit Red Wings in 1936 and '37. In the struggle to do it again, one thing they could count on was continuity. The 1947–48 Leafs featured much the same cast of characters, from top to bottom. Overseeing the whole operation was Conn Smythe's iron eye, and behind the bench was Hap Day's icy glare. On the ice, Syl Apps still captained the ship with elegance and leadership, Ted Kennedy led the youth movement in the forward ranks, and Turk Broda continued to anchor the net. The only change of significance was an early season trade with the Chicago Black Hawks that brought in Max Bentley, who'd led the league in points the previous season. With Bentley in the fold, the already potent Leafs were now a powerhouse to be reckoned with.

On defense, the Leafs were building a bulwark of experience and intelligence, with Jimmy Thomson, Gus Mortson, Wally Stanowski, and Garth Boesch. In Barilko, they'd added brute force with a latent but instinctive offensive flair. His late-season audition in 1946–47 had been impressive but uneven. He hit everything that moved but also some things that didn't, and he made the kinds of mistakes young defensemen inevitably do, chasing hits out of position and trying to do too much. He learned, often the hard way, that the NHL punished overzealousness with embarrassment.

This was supposed to be Barilko's settling season, and so he arrived at training camp more assured. The raw edge was still there, razor sharp and ready to bleed out the opposition, but it was now paired with something resembling patience. To earn a spot on the roster, Barilko knew he'd have to do more than just dish out violent bodychecks, so he'd spent the summer up in Timmins working hard to increase his speed and stabilize his balance while breaking in a new pair of skates. He came into camp faster and stronger on his feet. Even the press took note of the change. Barilko's serviceable, if inelegant, skating "technique" had evolved into a powerful stride that suddenly made him one of the faster players on the team.

The Leafs' defense was based on structure and simplicity, but it also relied on bravado. Barilko brought that in spades. He was a defenseman who made opposing forwards hesitate and created space for teammates simply by being on the ice.

"What else can I do to stay up in the big league?" Barilko said. "I'm not much of a skater, not much of a stickhandler, not much of a scorer. I have to be good for something, else I'm back in the leaky roof."

As the season progressed, Barilko gained more ice time. He didn't play defense like a surgeon. He played it like a demolition foreman. In a league where fear was currency, Barilko was getting rich off his bodychecks.

"You can feel it when it's a good one," he said. "I get a big bang out of it."

Yet there was more to Barilko's game than body contact. More than his skating had improved. He no longer handled the puck like it was a live grenade. He could rush it out of danger and, when needed, jump into the attack. In an era of defensive defensemen, Barilko began to show flashes of offensive upside.

But he was still a rookie prone to making rookie mistakes, sometimes in bunches. In a mid-November game against the Boston Bruins, Barilko was on the ice for six goals against in a 7–2 loss. Eleven days later, still stinging from the drubbing, he exacted some retribution on his favorite target, who would later have surgery to repair the damage done by Barilko.

"Milt Schmidt was coming up the boards," Barilko said. "He had deked one of our men. Then he deked another. Both times feinting for the middle of the rink and going through on the boards. I figured he'd try the same thing on me. He did. It was a terrific check."

In his first full NHL season, Barilko had to get used to the league's relentless schedule, long train rides, hard practices, and limited days off. But he embraced the grind. He wasn't flashy in the box score, but his impact was unmistakable. The crease was harder to access, the corners became hazardous territory, and the middle of the ice was almost entirely off limits.

By New Year's Day, the Leafs were in first place and Barilko was being mentioned in the Calder Trophy conversation for the season's top rookie, his eighteen games in the 1946–47 regular season having fallen under the twenty-game cutoff for eligibility. He was also on pace to break the NHL's single-season mark for penalty minutes, the 167 set by Leafs legend Red Horner in 1935–36.

"I don't mind getting a penalty when I have it coming," Barilko said. "Now, I think the referees are watching me too closely and are giving me chippy penalties. That's the only trouble with being the league's badman. That won't stop me, though. I like it here."

By now, Barilko had earned a new moniker. "Billy the Kid" just didn't do it anymore. In trying to describe his playing style, the press had taken to using various cognates of "bash" to describe Barilko's bodychecks. Eventually, the alliteration was just too tempting to ignore. He became "Bashin' Bill."

"Bob Gracie had me work on my backward skating, which in turn helped with my bodychecking," Barilko said. "There aren't too many trying to go through the center on me now. That cuts down their chances and makes me look better."

Off the ice, Barilko was slowly becoming a key element of the team's chemistry. Even as a rookie, he'd become comfortable enough to ham it up with the team's veterans rather than defer to them. Late in the season, after a low-scoring, penalty-filled 3–1 loss to the Bruins in Boston, the twenty-year-old rookie was playing rummy with a couple of thirtysomething veterans on the train ride home to Toronto and discussing why goals were down across the league.

"Only occasionally do you see a wide-open game with plenty of scoring opportunities," mused forward Nick Metz.

"Not only that but the goaltending is better," Broda added with a wink.

Never one to pass up a good quip, Barilko chirped his plump and balding goaltender, who was thirteen years his senior and near the end of a career that'd begun in 1936, when Barilko was just nine years old.

"You better think of retiring," Barilko told Broda with a smile. "Why, when I was a little punk you were in the nets for Leafs. You're going along on your name. I'm getting tired of stopping shots for you."

By the end of the regular season, the Leafs had secured first place, Broda had won the Vezina Trophy for the second time in his career, and Barilko had led the league in penalty minutes, just shy of Horner's all-time mark. He fell short of winning the Calder Trophy, but his five goals and nine assists for fourteen points were second among rookie defensemen in the league, behind only Red Kelly and ahead of Doug Harvey, both future Hall of Famers.

The Leafs entered the postseason as the favorites for the Stanley Cup, drawing the Bruins, who'd finished eighteen points back, in the semifinals. But the Bruins served notice that they weren't about to lay down for the more highly skilled Leafs. They were intent on turning the series into a grudge match, and it worked through most of the opening game. The Bruins held a two-goal lead midway through the third period, only to see it slip away with a pair of late goals by the Leafs. With the momentum swung their way, the Leafs completed the comeback with a 5–4 overtime win.

Two days later, after a practice ahead of the second game, the Leafs sat in their dressing room, cool and relaxed after their game one win. At one point, Kennedy pulled out a set of golf clubs he'd just bought. Teammates were taking turns swinging and assessing the woods and irons when Barilko walked over, picked up the driver, and looked it over.

"Boy, you could make a nice hole in a guy's head with this," he said.

After the Leafs took the second game 5–3, heads rolled when the series shifted to Boston. Barilko was a menace, punishing the Bruins with open-ice hipchecks and board-rattling bodychecks. With the Leafs leading 2–0, including a goal by Barilko, the Bruins, and their fans, had had enough of the impudent rookie. During play, Schmidt and defenseman Fern Flaman pinned Barilko over the sideboards, where two Bruins fans began raining punches down on the back of his head. None the worse for his front row experience, Barilko and the Leafs ran away with the penalty-filled affair in a 5–1 win to take a commanding lead in the series. The Bruins managed to squeak out a win in game four, but it would be the Leafs' only loss in the playoffs. They dispatched the Bruins in five games to set up a Stanley Cup Final showdown with the Red Wings.

If the regular season forged Barilko's confidence, the playoffs sharpened it. His game rose to meet the moment. He stood taller in front of Broda and elevated his physical play without crossing the line. He was never going to be the headline scorer, but he was part of every battle that made scoring possible by playing the kind of defense that didn't show up on scoresheets but won championships. Against the Wings, his work was on full display.

Barilko was everywhere throughout the final, taking two penalties in the first game, getting into a spirited fight in the second, and starting a wrestling match in the third after a Wings player struck a teammate over the head with his stick. The Leafs swept the series in four straight games after a decisive 7–2 win in Detroit in game four.

For the first time in the franchise's history, the Leafs had clinched back-to-back championships. In just a little over a year, Barilko had become a two-time Stanley Cup champion.

No one was calling him a fluke anymore. Indeed, Barilko's reputation had spread beyond Toronto. Opposing teams circled his number on lineup cards, forwards warned each other on the bench, and coaches planned around him. He'd become one of the league's most feared young defensemen. Within the Leafs' room, his influence was beginning to grow. He was never much of a talker. He led with his shoulders and that lethal left hip. He set a tone that matched the Leafs' identity and fit in not just stylistically but spiritually. In an era where teammates valued character as much as talent, that mattered. For fans and media, Barilko wasn't a story yet. He was simply there, night after night, hit after hit, rush after rush, shift after shift.

That second season was the hinge of his career. It was the year Barilko crossed the invisible line from potential to permanence, the year he proved he could handle the pressure of Toronto, the expectations of champions, and the rigor of the NHL schedule. The year he became, unmistakably, a Maple Leaf.

The Dynasty

Barilko was a tremendous hockey player, and would've been as tremendous a defenseman as had ever played the game.
—Howie Meeker, Toronto Maple Leafs teammate

I RISE FROM THE TILED underbelly of Union Station and walk into a short section of Toronto's 30-kilometer (18-mile) underground pedestrian network. A slow-moving human river of blue and white pulls me along the corridor toward the arena as the city narrows into a single shared pulse, albeit faint, for one last Saturday night this season. From somewhere ahead, a "Go, Leafs, Go!" chant ripples back toward me, both an acceptance of a failed present and a sustained hope for future glory. As the throng carries me along, I catch sight of a Bill Barilko jersey. Tonight, most jerseys in the crowd will be of Auston Matthews, William Nylander, and John Tavares. At every Toronto Maple Leafs game, though, there is always a Barilko, a player who suffuses an arena he never skated in with the fighting spirit his old team is trying so desperately to recover.

It is *Hockey Night in Canada* in Toronto in mid-April. For the past nine years, this would've been just a late-season tune-up for the Maple Leafs ahead of the playoffs. But after winning their division last season and then coming within one win of the conference finals, the Leafs have fallen to last place. Limping into town is the team that eliminated them, the defending two-time Stanley Cup champion Florida Panthers. Having been to the Stanley Cup Final three straight years and won the past two, the Panthers were on the cusp of becoming a dynasty until injuries drained their roster and dropped them to the bottom of the division alongside the Leafs. Before the start of the season, they were the favorites to win it all again, which would've made them just the sixth three-time consecutive champions in NHL history and the first in more than forty years.

I pick up my press pass and take the elevator up to the sixth floor to the Foster Hewitt Media Gondola. In the hallway, beside the room where the Leafs' extra players will take in the game, I walk past a photo of a suited Barilko doing an interview with a local radio station and then find my spot along the long row of seats for scribes and talking heads. Directly across from me, high above the ice, Barilko's banner hangs silently between that of his coach Hap Day and the player who would eventually take his place on the Leafs, Tim Horton. Most fans think this is Barilko's original banner. It is not. The original, returned to his hometown in 2016, resides above the ice at McIntyre Arena, where he freed himself from the fatalism of the mines to chart his own path aboveground. In February 1999, Barilko's original banner was lowered at Maple Leaf Gardens, driven a couple of miles down to its new home, here, adjoining Union Station, and then lifted into the rafters again. What began with reraising his banner in what was then called Air Canada Centre has extended to a replacement banner and an array of displays, photographs, artwork, and lyrics in the since-renamed Scotiabank Arena, all in honor of the franchise's famous fallen Leaf.

When the game gets underway, the Panthers take only twenty-three seconds to silence the already uninspired crowd. Five minutes later, they score again.

During the first intermission, with the Leafs down 2–0, I take the elevator to the main concourse at street level to an elaborate vertical glass display that holds a stick Barilko used from his last season with the Leafs and Gord Downie's framed handwritten lyrics to The Tragically Hip's "Fifty Mission Cap." This little shrine was set up this season in honor of Barilko's Stanley Cup–winning overtime goal seventy-five years ago. Had the Leafs made the playoffs, the organization would've held a celebration on or near the anniversary, April 21, 2026. Instead, with the Leafs long since eliminated, the day will pass without ceremony.

Early in the second period, the Panthers score again. The game is beginning to look like it'll be a blowout when Nylander responds with a pair of goals just over a minute apart to bring a little life into the building. Both teams are going through the motions, just hoping to get through the final few games of the season without any more injuries.

During a TV timeout, "Fifty Mission Cap" rips through the arena, as it does at just about every Leafs home game. I look around to see how many fans are making the connection to the anniversary and looking up at Barilko's banner. But most are looking down, buried in their phones, as Downie delivers the Coles Notes version of Barilko's story.

With the Panthers leading 3–2 into the second intermission, I take the elevator down to the third floor, where a screaming Downie and a smiling Barilko are pictured side by side above a heading that reads: A LEGEND INSPIRED BY A LEGEND. I continue down to the 200 level to ScotiaClub, one of several premium clubs scattered throughout the arena. On my way there, I pass an elaborate piece of artwork featuring layered headlines about Barilko's legacy:

> BARILKO GOAL STILL GOLD
>
> LEAF LEGEND'S STAR ON THE RISE AGAIN
>
> TRAGICALLY HIP'S HAUNTING TUNE PAYS HOMAGE TO LEAFS' BARILKO

Toward the far end of the club are some of the lyrics Downie penned to Barilko. Scrawled in a handwritten font, they run in one long line above a row of plush, red booths and mahogany tables:

> *Bill Barilko disappeared that summer, he was on a fishing trip. The last goal he ever scored won the Leafs the Cup. —the tragically hip*

The team could've used Barilko tonight, if only to put up something resembling a fight. Back in the press box for the third period, I watch as the lifeless Leafs gift wrap the Panthers a meaningless 6–2 win. I follow the trickle of media who've stayed to the end down into the bowels of the arena and over to the dressing rooms. On the wall outside the Leafs' room hang mini banners for every Leaf whose number has been retired, including Barilko's number 5, which he wore for only one season. Down the hall to the right, where adoring Leafs fans stand in wait behind a stanchion hoping to catch a glimpse of a passing player of the present, is the same photo of Barilko's knockout grin that is on the billboard outside Timmins welcoming people to his hometown.

Rather than follow the media to collect some clichés in the postgame scrums, I instead walk over to the hallway leading to the team's media center, where the Leafs hold their postgame press conferences. Flanked by photos of Wendel Clark on the left and Darryl Sittler on the right is one of Barilko dated April 16, 1949. In the sepia hush of the photo, the Stanley Cup rises like a polished altar. Beside it is Barilko, grinning with a quiet, knowing warmth, as if he alone understands the improbable path that brought it here.

To become a dynasty in the NHL is not merely to win repeatedly but to impose a stable identity on a team in which talent, time, and temperament align so perfectly that victory feels less like an achievement and more like destiny. It requires a core of transcendent players who evolve together and a cast of supporting players who are content to stay in the shadows so that the stars can shine. It involves a system that goes beyond tactics, outlives player turnover, and requires an organizational patience that resists both panic and complacency. A team must master not just the details of the game but the psychology of sustaining success. Each season is both a defense of the past and a reinvention of it, where the true achievement isn't dominance alone but the quiet, relentless normalization of excellence. Success becomes embedded in the institutional memory, passed along in the dressing room, from player to player, rather than constructed anew each season.

Just as the Panthers did this season, the Leafs entered the 1948–49 season as the two-time defending Stanley Cup champions and were favored to repeat the feat again. But dynasties aren't built on reputation alone. No team had yet to three-peat in the NHL's thirty-one years of existence. To become the first, the Leafs would have to maintain dominance without the longtime face of the franchise. After ten years in the league, all with the Leafs, Syl Apps was retiring at the top of his game as a Stanley Cup champion at only thirty-three years of age. Assuming the captaincy was twenty-two-year-old Ted Kennedy. Nick Metz retired as well, while Wally

Stanowski, Barilko's first defense partner with the Leafs, had been traded to the New York Rangers shortly after winning the Cup.

On defense, Garth Boesch and Bill Juzda, a fellow Ukrainian who came over in the trade with the Rangers, brought steadiness and positioning, while younger defensemen like Gus Mortson and Jimmy Thomson brought legs and hunger. Barilko brought intimidation and calculation, his main job to make life miserable for opposing forwards. Night after night, he did exactly that.

Just twenty-one years old when training camp opened in the fall, Barilko was still young by NHL standards, but he no longer played like a newcomer. The recklessness of his first two seasons with the Leafs had been tempered, though not entirely erased, as he slowly accumulated experience. He still hit harder than any other defenseman in the league, but there was a growing sense of timing in his game. He was learning when to step up, when to hold the line, and when to let the game come to him. Day began using him more and more in defensive situations, particularly against other teams' top lines. Slowly but surely, Barilko was earning his coach's trust.

After another summer of skating back home in Timmins, Barilko arrived at training camp in the fall of 1948 a sure thing to make the team. His increased status was shown in his new number. This was a time when a player's number reflected his standing in the team's hierarchy. Veterans wore the lowest numbers, rookies the highest. A lower number could net a player perks, a comfy lower berth in the sleeping car on an overnight train, for instance. No longer a rookie but not yet a veteran, Barilko could only inch down from number 21 to 19. It would take two more years for Barilko to finally grab the number 5 now commemorated in the Leafs' home arena.

In camp, too, was his brother, Alex. The Barilko boys got to face each other in an intrasquad game. It was the closest they would ever come to realizing their dream of playing together with the Leafs.

Barilko treated training camp like it was already the regular season. Several teammates fell to injury at his hand, or rather hip. The press started calling it getting "Barilkoed" or coming down with a bad case of "Barilkoitis." It was a condition that would infect the dressing rooms of the other five teams in the league throughout the season.

In one game against the Montreal Canadiens, both Ken Reardon and Norm Dussault were sent off on stretchers after getting Barilkoed. Against the Boston Bruins, Grant Warwick came down with a bad case of Barilkoitis after being driven headfirst into the boards with a cross-check that would've been an automatic suspension in today's NHL. The Detroit Red Wings weren't spared, either, as Barilko leveled George Gee, who'd just returned from a knee injury, and body-slammed Pete Horeck to the injured list.

Against the Chicago Black Hawks, Barilko added Bill Gadsby to his growing list of player patients, flattening the Black Hawks' star defenseman and nearly taking out one of his own teammates in the process. It came with only a couple of minutes left in a game in Chicago. With his team on the power play, Gadsby was being chased by the Leafs' Max Bentley while carrying the puck into the offensive zone. Barilko took a full twenty-foot run at Gadsby and met him at the blue line. The bodycheck reverberated throughout the arena and drew audible gasps from the crowd. Teammates later said it sounded like two freight trains colliding. Gadsby lay on the ice unconscious with a separated shoulder that would leave him with a permanent lump. Barilko didn't escape unscathed either. Stunned by the impact, he had to crawl back to the bench. The Hawks protested the violence of the hit to referee Bill Chadwick, who could only admire Barilko's handiwork.

"That's the best check I've ever seen," he said.

The impact was so hard that Barilko admitted the hit had "even winded me a bit," while Bentley was just glad he wasn't collateral damage.

"I looked up just in time to steer away before Barilko let go," Bentley said after the game. "If I ever got mixed up in that collision, I'd still be sailing through the air."

One of the ongoing storylines of Barilko's early career was discipline, or rather the lack of it. He played on the edge, and often beyond it. That edge was part of his effectiveness, and the Leafs understood that. But they also knew that penalties could swing games in a league where power plays lasted a full two minutes, regardless of whether the penalized team was scored upon. Day worked hard with Barilko to get him to channel his aggression. He still took penalties, but fewer of them were frivolous. Compared to the previous season, he would spend nearly a full hour less in the penalty box. It wasn't a total transformation, but it was a necessary one. Barilko was learning the hardest lesson for any physical defenseman: intimidation is most effective when it is predictable to your teammates and unpredictable to your opponents.

By then, opposing teams were beginning to adjust their game plans around Barilko's presence. Forwards were quicker to dump the puck into the Leafs' end instead of trying to challenge his side of the ice. Rather than risk an open-ice hit or a crushing check along the boards, wingers hesitated before cutting through the middle or trying to swing wide on Barilko. Coaches warned their players about staying too long in front of the Leafs' net, lest they return to the bench plucking splinters out of their backs from Barilko's lumber. This grudging respect didn't show up in headlines, but it had effect. In a tight, low-scoring league, creating a moment of hesitation could be the difference between a clean scoring chance and a harmless shot from the perimeter.

By midseason, the Leafs had yet to find their rhythm, going nearly a month without a win at one point and stringing together longer streaks of losses and ties than victories. Only three times had they managed to win back-to-back games, one being a pair of Turk Broda shutouts late in November. Like the team itself, Barilko had his ups and downs, his good games and bad games. For every bone-rattling bodycheck, sacrificial blocked shot, and timely rush up the ice, there was an overeager hit that took him out of position, a rushing forward that blew by him down the right wing, or a risky attempt to jump into the rush. In a 4–1 loss to the Canadiens in Toronto, he made a half-hearted effort to retrieve the puck in his own zone only to be stripped of it by the Canadiens' Billy Reay, who promptly put it behind Broda. But Barilko did show his slick retrieval skills in Chicago when he managed to chase down a rabbit after a Hawks fan released it right onto the ice during a game. Barilko's snare of the hare drew the loudest ovation of the night in a 2–0 shutout win for the Leafs.

As the regular season wound down, Barilko had become public enemy number one around the league. Gadsby, Warwick, Reardon, Dussault, Gee, Horeck, and Milt Schmidt had all been Barilkoed and sent to the injured list. Then, in the Leafs' final game, in Boston, with the Bruins comfortably ahead 7–2, Barilko put Warwick out again with another hard late-game bodycheck. When the crowd started throwing their displeasure at Barilko in the penalty box, the referee sent him off the ice. Barilko did just that, smiling as showers of programs and peanuts rained down on him while he made his way to the dressing room.

After finishing first the previous season, the Leafs were life and death to make the playoffs in 1949, falling to fourth with a losing record. The only reason they were even able to secure the final playoff spot was because the Hawks had the league's worst defense and couldn't take advantage of the Leafs having lost five of their final six games. Player turnover upset them, injuries hobbled them, and inconsistency dogged them. If they couldn't string three wins together all season long, how could they win their third Stanley Cup in a row?

The 1949 playoffs opened against a familiar foe, as the Leafs faced the Bruins in the semifinals, a matchup defined by physical play and stubborn defense. These weren't games for highlight reels. These were wars of attrition.

But before the battle had begun, Barilko was already observing his annual postseason superstition. For whatever reason, Barilko equated the length of the Leafs' annual playoff run to how long he let his fingernails grow. During the return trip home after winning the first two games in Boston, which also featured an impromptu birthday celebration for the young defenseman, a reporter asked Barilko why he hadn't cut his cuticles.

"What, cut them and cut our luck?" he replied. "I haven't touched them since before the first Boston playoff game."

He wouldn't for three more weeks.

The Leafs would lose game three but would go on to beat the Bruins in five games to set up a showdown with the first-place Red Wings. But the rival Canadiens had done the Leafs a favor, taking the Wings the distance in their semifinal matchup. The Wings would ultimately prevail in seven close games, but their vaunted offense could muster no more than three goals in any of them against a stingy Canadiens defense.

While the Canadiens were wearing out the Wings in their hard-fought seven-game series, Conn Smythe had taken the Leafs down to St. Catharines, where his players could prepare for the final away from the prying eyes of the public. It'd taken all sixty games of the regular season, but the Leafs had finally found their swagger with their five-game destruction of the Bruins.

Coming into the Stanley Cup Final, the well-rested Leafs went to

Detroit after an eight-day layoff to face a weary Wings team that only had two days to recover after barely squeaking past the Canadiens. By the time the final opened, the Leafs were champing at the bit to get on the ice and get after the Wings, strutting with the knowledge that they'd swept them the year before and already had them gassed before the puck had even dropped for the final.

"It's going to be a tough series," Barilko said before it began. "I don't want to go out on a limb, but we'll sure be trying to take 'em in four straight, as we did last season."

It was a bold prediction but also a telling one. After losing only six games in Detroit all season, the Wings were quick to drop the first two at home in Olympia Stadium. Not wanting to let the Wings back into the series as it shifted to Toronto, the Leafs went to work, surgically deconstructing the Wings' high-octane offense. On the rare occasion the Wings did get to Broda, the Leafs' veteran goaltender turned them away. Visibly frustrated, all the Wings could muster were five total goals, while the Leafs scored three in every game. Once again, the Leafs swept the Wings in four straight games to win the Stanley Cup.

Three championships in three years. For Barilko, it was destiny continued. For the Leafs, it was a dynasty realized.

As the Leafs celebrated on the ice, photographers snapped photos of the NHL's first dynasty. In one photo, Barilko leans in beside the Stanley Cup as teammates hover in a loose constellation, their faces caught between pride and fatigue, some peering over shoulders, others half-lost in shadow, as though unsure whether to bask in the moment or simply collapse into it. In the foreground, coach Day and NHL president Clarence Campbell clasp hands with the solemn acknowledgment of diplomats concluding a treaty, their handshake intruding upon the scene like a misplaced ceremony, oblivious, almost comically so, to the presence of something far greater. Behind them all, history settles quietly into place. A third straight Stanley Cup triumph, the first of its kind in the NHL, while Barilko, smiling beside the Cup, seems already to belong to legend rather than the hallway to the media room in Scotiabank Arena, where the photo hangs today.

Bill Barilko (top left and right) with brother Alex and mother Faye (bottom left) and sister Anne (bottom right).
Courtesy of the Klisanich Family Collection

Barilko relaxes during his annual summer fishing excursions around Timmins.

Barilko poses with movie star and official team mascot Vera-Ellen during his time with the Hollywood Wolves.
Courtesy of the Klisanich Family Collection

Barilko strolls the streets of Hollywood with his brother, Alex, during their time in the Pacific Coast Hockey League.
Courtesy of the Klisanich Family Collection

Barilko warms up before a game at Maple Leaf Gardens.
Courtesy of Bill Hunter

Barilko in 1948 (top) and with Louise Hastings and friends in 1949 (bottom).
Courtesy of the Klisanich Family Collection

Toronto Maple Leafs president Conn Smythe congratulates Barilko after he scored his overtime goal (top), and Barilko's mother ladles champagne for her son after the game (bottom).
Courtesy of the City of Toronto Archives

Dr. Henry Hudson's Fairchild 24 rests on Porcupine Lake in Timmins in 1950, one summer before the fateful fishing trip.
Photo by Elvin Black

Helicopter pilot Gary Fields was the first to spot the wreckage in 1962.
Photo by the Ontario Department of Lands and Forests

Dr. John Shaw, who took over Dr. Hudson's dental practice, stands by one of the pontoons and the sign he put up in 2005, in honor of Barilko and Hudson (top left). The wreckage was airlifted out from the crash site in 2011 (top right).
Courtesy of the Timmins Sports Heritage Hall of Fame

Steve Paikin and Ronnie Shuker (third and fourth from left), along with Chad Calaiezzi and Mark Fera (far right), set out for the crash site in 2026 with a documentary film crew.
Courtesy of Brian Jones

Barilko welcomes people to Timmins from his billboard east of the city opposite Porcupine Lake, where the plane departed and never returned.
Courtesy of Ronnie Shuker

A piece of street art in Toronto pays tribute to Barilko and his legendary overtime goal.
Courtesy of Ronnie Shuker

The Year between Banners

Barilko is the hardest hitter in the league. When he hits you, he hurts you.

—Elmer Lach, Montreal Canadiens forward

AFTER RUMBLING EAST ACROSS the Bloor Street Viaduct to Toronto's east end, I exit the subway at Pape Station and walk to my old stomping grounds here in Greektown. In my seven years here, I never knew Bill Barilko had lived and once worked right in the heart of the neighborhood on Danforth Avenue. During the hockey season, he would drive from his room at the Eton House, just recently demolished, across the viaduct over the Don Valley, and then down to the corner of Church and Carlton, where he would ply his winter trade at Maple Leaf Gardens. In summer, after the NHL season had wrapped up, he would simply walk the few blocks west to his new side hustle near Broadview Avenue.

The summer of 1949 was the first that Barilko didn't spend most of it in Timmins. Instead, he took a room at the Eton House to be close to his new business venture. In the NHL of the 1940s, players were considered little more than cattle to league executives and team owners. There was no players' association, no one looking out for the players' interests. Contracts were rarely negotiated. They were take-it-or-leave-it unilateral deals, and most players just took it. So in the offseason, they had to supplement their meager salaries with summer work.

For Barilko and his brother, Alex, who'd been playing with the Toronto Marlboros, a local senior amateur club, that meant starting up Barilko Bros. From their appliance store, they sold just about every electrical contrivance available at the time: televisions, radios, stoves, phonographs, lamps, laundry machines, toasters, vacuums, alarm clocks, fans. The brothers even dabbled in their favorite summer pastime, offering fishing tackle and angling supplies, including province-wide delivery of live bait like worms, frogs, crawfish, and leeches.

Today, sandwiched between a real estate office and a bar, the location, at 167 Danforth Avenue, is home to a boutique law firm. Standing amid teetering stacks of files, chairs half-turned as though left abruptly in mid-conversation, and a coatrack waiting patiently for lives that come and go, I have a hard time imagining this place once filled with early TV sets, postwar appliances, and fishing lures.

From down the hall, John Lister welcomes me in and gestures for us to sit at a matching olive-green sofa and love seat in front of a large table awash in magazines. Between Toronto Maple Leafs fan pages, forums, social media accounts, and random blogs and vlogs, I'd found a number of comments from Barilko fans who said they'd stopped in here at his old store on the Danforth, enough for me to come myself and ask John about them.

"Bill Barilko?" he says. "This is the first time I've ever heard his name. I should be more aware of hockey history, but I'm not a hockey guy."

"Not everyone has to be," I reply.

John has worked here for thirty-one years. In all that time, he says, he's never seen anyone come into the office asking about Barilko nor have any of his colleagues mentioned one doing so. Although he hasn't heard of Barilko, he is curious, so he peppers me with questions. I recap the story for him: the goal, the fishing trip, the disappearance, the discovery, the songs, and the old appliance store he used to run here with his brother. About all that's left from then, all that connects Barilko's store to the law office, is the original red brick of the building, sandblasted and restored in the early 1980s.

"This is great brick, best feature of the whole place," John says. "This is just a boring old office now. Long way from an appliance store."

John's partner grew up in Smooth Rock Falls, about an hour north of Timmins, so we quickly fall into conversation about Northern Ontario, the Polar Bear Express train that runs from Cochrane to Moosonee at the southern edge of James Bay, and our respective experiences of minus 50°C (minus 58°F) weather there. When it is time for me to leave, I thank John for his time, and we exchange business cards. Before going, I ask him what type of law he practices.

"I do wills and estates," he says. "Do you have a will?"

I don't. But I'm in my fifties now, and probably should, so I make plans to come back. No one knows when the other side will come calling for them.

"Bill Barilko," John says to himself as I leave. "What a remarkable story."

Back when the place became Barilko Bros., the brothers held a grand opening and took out ads in local newspapers. Teammates came out in support, and fans flocked to the event, bringing traffic along Danforth Avenue to a standstill as goods flew out the door. Even Conn Smythe couldn't leave empty-handed.

"I signed my contract this week," Barilko said, "and also sold Mr. Smythe a television set and a refrigerator."

Before training camp, Barilko was able to get back to Timmins for one outdoor adventure that summer. Fellow defenseman Gus Mortson had been prospecting for years in the bush north of Timmins and had invited Barilko to come along in search of uranium. Their teammates had a good laugh at their expense when the two announced their plans at a team dinner before the 1949 final.

"Mortson just wants to use you as a pack horse on those long hauls through the bush," Jimmy Thomson said to Barilko.

"That's all right with me," Barilko replied. "I'll carry forty pounds of equipment all day. Keep me in shape for next season."

"You think you're going to look for uranium," Baz Bastien said to Mortson. "But if you take Barilko, you'll be looking for Barilko all the time."

"Gosh, I hope we don't get lost," Barilko said.

"Never got lost yet," Mortson replied. "Touch wood."

When October arrived, the assumption, and expectation, was that the Maple Leafs would once again find their way to the top of the NHL by season's end. But the 1949–50 season would test the Leafs in ways they hadn't been since Barilko first arrived in Toronto on that wintry night in early February 1947. The Leafs entered the season as the league's gold standard. Smythe's roster was deep, balanced, and battle-hardened, with Hap Day's steadying hand still behind the bench. Max Bentley was again one of the team's top scorers, Ted Kennedy remained the emotional and competitive engine up front, and Turk Broda continued to loom large in goal. On the back end, the Leafs relied on their usual blend of ruggedness and intelligence, and Barilko, who'd put on ten pounds of muscle during the offseason, was right at the heart of it.

When told earlier in the summer that the league had approved a seventy-game regular season schedule, adding ten more games for the already overworked and underpaid players, he quipped, surely to the chagrin of both Smythe and Day, "We'll just have fewer practices."

Before the season started, Barilko told his teammates he'd give any player a free TV from his appliance store for scoring a hat trick or one to Broda for posting a shutout. Less than a month into the season, Broda already had his TV, as did Harry Watson, after scoring three goals in an 8–1 win over the Boston Bruins. When a reporter suggested his wager could prove expensive over the course of an entire season, Barilko shot back, "But it will be worth it!"

The Leafs started the season strong, losing only once in their first eight games and taking hold of first place after Barilko scored twice in a 4–2 win over the New York Rangers. But things started to unravel when he sustained an early-season knee injury after knocking Clare Martin of the Detroit Red Wings unconscious with a bodycheck. The injury kept Barilko out of the lineup for three weeks. His absence showed. Without Barilko, the Leafs lost five of their next six games. They needed their basher back.

But before Barilko could be cleared to play, he first had to endure Day's conditioning drills. He all but crawled off the ice and onto the training table in the dressing room afterward.

"The knee didn't bother me," Barilko said. "But, oh brother, that whip. The coach had me racing back and forth across the rink, and at the end I could hardly see where I was going."

After missing eleven games, during which the Leafs went 4–6–1, Barilko made his return to the lineup against the Montreal Canadiens at home in Toronto. The Leafs managed a 2–2 tie, but Barilko clearly looked rusty after three weeks away, as Richard, Lach, and the Canadiens' other high-flying forwards repeatedly blew by him.

It took a while for Barilko to find his legs again and for the Leafs to find their rhythm. They won just twelve of their first thirty-five games, going seven games without a win at one point and then, later, twelve games with only one victory. It wasn't until the calendar flipped to a new decade that Barilko and the Leafs finally found their game.

When he was in the lineup, Barilko anchored a defense that prided itself on predictability and reliability. Although his offensive numbers look modest in retrospect, he put up the best scoring statistics of his career, with seven goals and ten assists for seventeen points, including a nifty goal against the Chicago Black Hawks on the only penalty shot of his career. He was tops among Leafs defensemen in both goals and points, and fourth and eighth league-wide among all rear guards. It is no coincidence that he registered the fewest penalty minutes of his three full seasons to date.

Barilko continued to send opponents to the injured list, including a shoulder injury to Ken Reardon (again) of the Canadiens, an Achilles tendon tear to Ed Sandford of the Bruins, and a beatdown of the Canadiens' Hal Laycoe, who grazed Barilko's blond mane as he slashed at a loose puck and received the defenseman's most ill-willed intentions in response, as Barilko came up chucking rights and lefts that knocked Laycoe's glasses off his face and forced him out of the game. Whenever Barilko was on the ice, opposing forwards quickly learned to keep their head up and on a swivel.

"You always have to keep one eye on Barilko," said Black Hawks forward Bep Guidolin, "or he'll flatten you like a pancake."

By midseason, the Leafs had dropped to fifth place, just two points ahead of the cellar-dwelling Hawks and a full eighteen points behind the first-place Red Wings, who were running away with the league. After his knee injury healed, nothing could keep Barilko out of the lineup, not even a three-digit fever ahead of a crucial game in New York against the

Rangers late in the season with a playoff spot still in doubt. He popped some penicillin pills and played, even notching an assist and taking a penalty in a 5–2 loss.

One of the subtler stories of the 1949–50 season was the evolution of the Leafs' defense corps. Injuries and lineup adjustments forced new pairings and new responsibilities. Barilko found himself paired with different partners over the course of the season, adapting his game to complement whoever lined up beside him. If his partner was more offense-minded, Barilko stayed home. If his partner needed defensive support, Barilko provided it. That adaptability made him invaluable, especially as the season wore on and fatigue set in.

Yet even with Barilko's consistency, the Leafs weren't quite the same team that had steamrolled its way to three straight Stanley Cup championships. Other teams were improving. The Wings, in particular, were emerging as the Leafs' most serious rival, a relentless club that matched them stride for stride. It took a strong second-half push, including a stretch of twelve wins in fifteen games, for the Leafs to climb into third place.

When the playoffs arrived, a matchup against those first-place Wings was in order. The Leafs were still strong, but they were no longer overwhelming. Where the Leafs relied on structure, discipline, and experience, the Wings countered with pace, precision, and firepower. They were fast, skilled, and hungry, and in Ted Lindsay, Sid Abel, and Gordie Howe they had the league's top three leaders in points on their first line. Unfortunately for the Wings, they would have to do without one of them early in the playoffs.

The Leafs looked like they'd found their championship form early with a decisive 5–0 shutout win in Detroit in the first game of the series, with Barilko scoring a goal, adding an assist, taking three penalties, and getting into a late-game dustup to lead the way. But few cared much for the score. Everyone was talking about Howe, who'd fallen awkwardly into the boards at center ice and struck his head on the dasher while trying to make a hit on Kennedy. Howe was lifted off the ice on a stretcher, bleeding profusely, and taken to the hospital, where he had emergency surgery to relieve pressure in his skull. He sustained a fractured skull, a broken cheekbone and nose, various lacerations, and a concussion.

From then on, with Howe out of the lineup, the Wings and Leafs traded victories until the series was all tied at three wins each. Each game had been a study in tension. Momentum swung back and forth, never settling long enough for either team to feel like it had a grip on the series. For Barilko, the games had been a test of endurance and discipline. He played like the embodiment of both, but hockey is unforgiving. Even perfect positioning can be undone by a bounce, a deflection, a momentary lapse.

Game seven, in Detroit, arrived with all the weight elimination games carry. For the Leafs, it was an opportunity to continue a dynasty. For the Wings, it was a chance to end something that'd seemed preordained. Through three periods, neither team had found the back of the net. For the fourth time in the series, the Leafs had managed to shut out the powerful Wings through regulation. Ordinarily, that would've been enough to win any series, but nothing ever goes according to script in the playoffs. Now in overtime, the first goal of the game would be the series winner.

The two teams had already waded through one overtime epic in Toronto. In game four, the series had turned on a harmless shot from Wings defenseman Leo Reise that caromed off Mortson's shinpad just thirty-eight seconds into the second overtime. From the penalty box, where he sat helplessly after taking a slashing penalty, Barilko could only watch as the puck slid past Broda and the Toronto crowd deflated around him.

Now, in the dying tension of the final game of the series, with overtime dragging toward its midpoint and every shift carrying the weight of history, it was Reise again. From nearly the same spot on the ice where he'd broken the hearts of Leafs fans back in Toronto, Reise wound up and drove the puck toward the Leafs' net.

As the puck sailed somewhere toward him, Broda strained to see through the churning wall of bodies that swallowed his sight line, while Barilko fought to reclaim the blue paint, shoving, hacking, and sweeping at anything that threatened his goalie's crease. Legs tangled with skates, sticks clashed and whipped through the air, and exhausted players wrestled for inches of ice. Somewhere inside the chaos, the puck vanished. For one suspended heartbeat, it belonged to no one. Then fate found Barilko. Reise's shot struck his shinpad and caromed in an instant. Screened from the release and betrayed by the deflection, Broda never saw it coming. Before he could seal the gap, the puck slipped through the sliver of daylight between his skate and the post, turning Barilko's desperate attempt to save the moment into the cruel touch that doomed it.

For a moment, there was only silence on the Leafs' bench, the stunned, hollow silence that comes when a dynasty realizes that destiny has left it. Then came the roar within Olympia Stadium, rising like thunder through the arena.

The Leafs' Stanley Cup reign was over.

The Overtime Series

I hate that Barilko so much. I sure wish we had him with the Canadiens.
—Frank Selke, Montreal Canadiens general manager

AFTER A SLOW CRAWL through a construction-narrowed, traffic-worn stretch of Davenport Road in Toronto, I find a prime parking spot on a side street opposite a large industrial property just shy of Caledonia Park Road, the kind you grab without hesitation before someone else does. I step out into the sharp city air and walk past a row of two-story houses toward an old industrial corridor in the edgelands of the city's Earlscourt neighborhood. Beneath the railway underpass, the city seems to briefly dip and darken as I walk along the road toward the tracks amid the rumble of passing cars. There, along a cold concrete wall, leaves and litter along its base, a graffiti-art mural emerges in a storm of gray, white, and deep Toronto Maple Leafs blue. A player is frozen mid-dive, his body fully extended in that impossible moment between risk and glory. Above him, the words "1951 Stanley Cup Final" cut through the paint, while a crude, layered tag beneath him anchors the whole scene in legend:

BARILKO SCORES

Nicknamed the Canadian Mount Rushmore of Hockey, the mural is part of a larger effort to bring color and identity to an otherwise overlooked stretch of the city, celebrating the golden age of Canadian hockey and its mythic figures: Wayne Gretzky, Bobby Orr, Guy Lafleur, Doug Gilmour, Paul Henderson, Don Cherry, even Lord Stanley himself. Standing here in this quiet, dirty corner of the city, it feels like I've stumbled upon a shrine. More than one hundred feet wide, the mural is something makeshift, a piece of urban folk art and, for that reason, sacred, a place where history hasn't faded but simply settled into the wall. Bill Barilko's 1951 overtime goal echoes silently through the image, his story suspended in the damp midday air. I can almost feel the sudden lift of a crowd that isn't present, the ghost of Maple Leafs triumph pressed into the concrete.

Until Leo Reise's unlucky shot off his shinpad, all Barilko had known was victory and Stanley Cup success. Now, failure had finally found him.

When the hard luck of that deflection in Detroit carried over into 1950–51, turning it into a regular season filled with bad luck and bad decisions, Barilko found himself in unfamiliar territory. Injuries befell him, his coach benched him, threats of demotion dogged him, trade rumors followed him, reporters questioned his mojo, and potential replacements lurked in the background. All he'd worked so hard to earn suddenly seemed to be slipping away.

The team itself had entered the 1950–51 season with the inevitability of major changes that come after playoff disappointment. Conn Smythe still helmed the entire operation. But behind the bench, "Gentleman" Joe Primeau, who'd spent seven seasons as a Leaf in the 1930s, was brought in as coach to replace Hap Day, who'd been promoted to assistant general manager. In net, rookie goaltender Al Rollins, despite having just two games of NHL experience, was brought in to tandem with Turk Broda at a time when carrying two goalies was a luxury teams generally weren't willing to spend on. On defense, the team lost one of its regulars when Garth Boesch decided to return to life on the family farm in Saskatchewan. Together, Boesch and Barilko had formed what the press had dubbed the "Maginot Line," a defensive maneuver the two defensemen devised in which they would drop to their knees alongside each other to block shots. With Boesch retiring, that left Gus Mortson, Jimmy Thomson, Bill Juzda, and Barilko to anchor the defense corps, along with a hotshot prospect by the name of Hugh Bolton.

"Despite the loss of Garth Boesch, I think our defense will be as good as it was last year," Barilko said at training camp. "Bill Juzda and I proved we could work well together, and Hugh Bolton will help considerably."

When Barilko arrived at camp, he did so as a seasoned and successful veteran knowing his spot on the team was secure. Just four seasons into his NHL career, he'd already lived a hockey life fuller and far more successful than most players. He was only twenty-three, but he carried with him the crowning achievements of three Stanley Cup championships and had established himself as the NHL's roughest and toughest defenseman and the league's hardest hitter. But Barilko was more than just a brutalizing bodychecker. Few noticed it then, and no one has taken note since, but quite under the radar he'd quietly become one of the league's best goal-scoring defensemen. Coming off the best statistical season of his career, he'd begun to layer offensive instincts on top of his rugged defensive foundation. He'd developed a knack for arriving late in the offensive zone, drifting slowly into open space high in the slot, unbeknownst to defenders, ready to pounce on a rebound or a loose puck.

So, it was no surprise when Barilko unveiled a new trick at training camp. Little more than a gimmick to coaches, including Primeau, who demurred when told that Barilko had been working on it all summer long, the slap shot was a rarely used weapon in NHL back then, but Barilko had sought it out to add to his growing offensive arsenal.

"It's a deadly shot," he said, "mainly because it's low and hurried."

By then in his career, Barilko was counted on to set a physical tone for the Leafs. Against teams like the Montreal Canadiens and Detroit Red Wings, who boasted top-end offensive talent in Maurice Richard and Gordie Howe, Barilko's heavy checks sent a message early in games that life wouldn't be easy for them over the next sixty minutes. He didn't intimidate recklessly. His hits were precise and calculated. The best ones were perfectly timed, separating opponents from the puck and sometimes from their souls.

Against the Canadiens, his battles with Richard were legendary. Richard's speed and explosive release made him a nightmare for defensemen, but Barilko relished the challenge. He checked the Rocket relentlessly, using body position and leverage to force him wide, instead of allowing him to cut into the middle on his off wing, like Richard was wont to do, then punishing him along the boards. Against the Red Wings, Barilko often drew the assignment of dealing with Howe, a unicorn of strength and skill who could beat a team on the scoreboard just as easily as in the alley. Their collisions echoed through Maple Leaf Gardens in Toronto and Olympia Stadium in Detroit. They were two young titans testing the other's limits.

But in hockey, the bill eventually must be paid. The toll of Barilko's playing style had begun to exact a price on his body. After starting the season with a loss at home to the lowly Chicago Black Hawks and then eking out a tie in Detroit with the Wings, the Leafs beat the Bruins in Boston for their first win of the season. It was a costly victory for Barilko, who'd taken fourteen minutes in penalties, missed scoring a guaranteed goal, and ended up on the injured list for three games with a knee injury when he laid out Paul Ronty with the hardest hit of the game. This followed on a sore heel sustained on a blocked shot late in training camp and an elbow injury suffered against the Wings. The superstitious Barilko was beginning to think that changing his number from 19 to 5 before the season had been a mighty mistake.

"I didn't have any luck in training camp and now this," Barilko said of his knee injury. "Not only that, but I hurt my elbow against Detroit and missed a sure goal against Boston by firing over the net."

Like others in his era, Barilko played through injuries that would sideline most players today. He believed deeply in duty, to the team, to the city, to the game itself. When today's players are lauded for their toughness, they're looked upon as throwbacks, old-school players who wear scars proudly. Barilko is their archetype. He received stitches between and even within periods, only to return to the ice posthaste. Broken noses, black eyes, aching ribs, none of them deterred him. This toughness enhanced his mystique. Fans adored him for his willingness to endure. In a city that valued grit as much as flair, Barilko embodied the ideal Maple Leaf.

Since joining the Leafs, Barilko had missed only fourteen regular season games and had played in every playoff game. After coming up from Hollywood late in the 1946–47 season, he didn't miss a game the rest of the way. In 1947–48, he missed only three, and in 1948–49 he played in every contest. By the 1949–50 season, when the NHL moved to a seventy-game schedule, the wear and tear of the NHL grind finally caught up to him, as he missed eleven games dealing with hand and arm injuries, a sprained ankle, and a charley horse. In 1950–51, he would miss twelve more over the course of the season.

When he returned from his knee injury ten days later, Barilko wasted no time making his presence felt. Jackie McLeod of the New York Rangers was one of the first to feel it, sent out on a stretcher with a broken collarbone and head injuries when Barilko folded him like a worthless poker hand, checking him face-first into the boards and knocking him unconscious. What would've been a guaranteed suspension today went unpenalized by the referee and unpunished by the league in 1950. McLeod spent the next three days in hospital. He played parts of three more seasons with the Rangers but was never the same after the hit.

The Leafs were the beneficiaries of Barilko's hard-nosed play, having gone eleven games without a loss before that game in New York and then going another nine games without a defeat shortly after adding defenseman Fern Flaman in a mid-November trade with the Bruins. As winter deepened, the Leafs settled into a familiar rhythm. By the halfway mark of the season, they were jockeying with the Wings for first place, well ahead of the other four teams. At one point, the Leafs even had the top four scorers in the league. Barilko, however, was beginning to struggle. His hard hitting had abated, his decision-making had become shaky, his playmaking erratic. The press had taken notice of the dramatic dip in his game:

Barilko was off his game all the way.

Leafs' defense was inept, particularly Barilko.

Barilko has been a big disappointment this season.

In a game in late December against the Bruins, Primeau sent his struggling rear guard a clear communiqué. Barilko dressed and was listed on the lineup sheet but didn't see a single shift, spending the entire game on the bench. A month later, against the Rangers, Primeau sent Barilko the same not-so-subtle missive, putting him in uniform but stapling him to the bench all game again. Neither message got through.

By then, Barilko's play had hit its nadir. Against the Black Hawks a day later, he took a foolish penalty in the middle of the first period. Primeau benched him for the rest of the game. Somehow, Barilko missed the memorandum yet again. The very next game, he was sent to the penalty box four times. At least Primeau took it in stride this time. After all, Barilko had tried hard.

"So hard that he got four penalties," Primeau said, laughing.

Off the ice, it was well known that Barilko, tall, blond, blue-eyed, with a winter white smile, was the most eligible bachelor on the team. Pricked with a touch of dandyism from his Hollywood days, he was proud of his sartorial splendor, owning more than forty suits and upward of a hundred ties. He was spending an inordinate amount of time at the racetrack and was working on opening a second store with his brother. People wondered if it was all affecting his game.

Speculation soon started circulating of Barilko getting demoted to Pittsburgh to play for the Hornets of the American Hockey League, the team and league he'd bypassed on his way to the Leafs back in February 1947. There were also rumors of a potential trade to Chicago, with Barilko going to the Hawks along with Rollins and Ray Timgren in return for goalie Harry Lumley. (During the playoffs, another rumor would surface of Barilko being traded to Montreal.) Smythe vehemently denied the gossip, calling it "one of the most amazing rumors of a hockey trade." But his response was notable for what he didn't deny. It was admission by omission.

"I don't know how such a rumor could get started," Smythe said, feigning ignorance like a flummoxed general manager of today. "I wouldn't trade Al Rollins for Harry Lumley even, and there's nobody I know who can take Ray Timgren's place."

Not a word about Barilko. He'd indeed been on the block.

Yet amid all the rumors, Barilko began to find his rhythm again by mid-February. After scoring only once to that point of the season, he suddenly rediscovered his scoring touch, notching four goals in five games to close out the month before torn ligaments in his ankle forced him to miss another three games in early March. As the season entered its final stretch, and the games piled up, injuries accumulated up and down the lineup. But Barilko only seemed to grow stronger as the season grew longer and the games more consequential. If anything, he appeared energized by the pressure, the compression of the schedule, and the urgency of the playoff race. Late in the season, *The Hockey News* named him player of the week in a laudatory column:

> *Barilko seems to be coming out of what up until now has been termed a rather disappointing season. The usually solid, hard-hitting rear guard hasn't been playing his regular game, and it's no secret that many fans, and also the Toronto front office, were rather surprised. But now it looks like the blond bombshell is coming out of his shell.*
>
> *On the blueline, Barilko is far from nice. In fact, if you look up they'll tell you that he is very dangerous. He has sidelined more players since he came into the NHL than any other three players put together. Opposing skaters have taken a decided dislike to him on the ice, for they know that he has no sympathy for them, be they rookies or ten-year veterans.*
>
> *The Leafs have always been rated a money team. When the chips are down and they have their work cut out for themselves, they seldom fail. That is what has made them so great in the past five seasons. And one of the main reasons for their greatness is Bashin' Bill Barilko.*

By the final weeks of the regular season, the old Barilko was back. There was no hint of fragility, no suggestion of endings, no indecision born of distraction, only the rugged defenseman fans had come to love and the team had come to depend on. As the Leafs finished on a seven-game winning streak, Barilko delivered some of his finest performances. The games felt like postseason previews. They were tight, tense, unforgiving, and Barilko thrived in them. Among them was a home game against the Canadiens in which Richard, with whom Barilko had engaged in an ongoing feud since his first NHL game, was given a headfirst and bloodied introduction to the Leafs' goalpost after the Rocket failed to heed Barilko's warnings about streaking too close to Rollins in the Leafs' net.

The Leafs finished just six points back of the first-place Wings but a full thirty points ahead of the Canadiens and thirty-three ahead of the Bruins, whom they'd meet again to start the playoffs. For Barilko, it'd been a trying season. His six goals and six assists for twelve points fell short of his career highs set the season prior. But with the playoffs coming, he had a clear road to redemption ahead of him as hockey's second season, the real season, began.

Barilko turned twenty-four just three days before the start of the playoffs and was playing the best hockey of his life. The Leafs were no longer defending champions, no longer the league's undisputed kings. They were contenders, chasing down the champs to reclaim their crown. Playoff hockey in the Original Six era was an unforgiving crucible. The margins were thinner, the hits harder, the ice tighter. But Barilko's game was built for spring.

The Leafs' semifinal series was a test of endurance rather than a spectacle. Six games of trench warfare defined by territorial battles were right up the battle-hardened Barilko's alley. Ahead of the first game of the series, coach Primeau cautioned his charges against taking the Bruins too lightly. Barilko, however, knew the importance of keeping things light under the weight of heavy expectations. Before the start of the series, Primeau had devised a "Fat Boy's Calorie Chart," as he titled it, specifically for Broda, who at just five-foot-nine but a plump 180 pounds promoted his girth as a shot-stopping strategy. Smythe, however, had benched Broda the season prior for being overweight, creating an off-ice soap opera that the press had dubbed the "Battle of the Bulge." Barilko joked that the team's playoff chances hinged as much on Broda's ability to count calories on Primeau's chart as they did on him saving shots.

"You might say we have a mathematical chance for the Cup," Barilko said to Broda, laughing. "If we'd had this last year, you wouldn't have been mixed up in the Battle of the Bulge."

Broda didn't start the series, but he was called into action before the end of the first period in game one when Rollins was injured in a collision with Pete Horeck and the Bruins leading 1–0. Broda allowed only one goal the rest of the game, but the Leafs couldn't create any offense. Even though the Bruins hadn't won any of the seven games they'd played at Maple Leaf Gardens all season long, they managed to come away with a 2–0 shutout victory.

In the second game, Barilko was all over the scoresheet and all over the Bruins. His long-distance screen shot early in the first period through a maze of players gave the Leafs their first goal of the playoffs and opened the scoring. He also visited the penalty box five times for twenty-one minutes in penalties, including three minors and a five-minute major, as well as a ten-minute misconduct after using his stick to provide referee Red Storey with a visual image of his disagreement on a call he'd made. The Bruins tied the game in the second period, and the teams marched through the rest of regulation toward overtime. It was then that Barilko did his most brutal work. Bodychecks sent Dunc Fisher off the ice on a stretcher for twelve stitches and Horeck off the ice for ten. Barilko also gave him a badly blackened eye for good measure. More Bruins would've likely been Barilkoed had the game not been called off with the teams still tied after the first overtime period. A municipal bylaw forbade sports games from being played past 11:45 p.m. on Saturday nights. Strangely, the league determined that the stats would count even though the score wouldn't. So, while Barilko got to keep his crooked stat line, the Leafs headed to Boston down a game in the series.

With three of the next four games in their own arena, the Bruins knew they would have to close out the series on home ice if they had any chance of advancing to the final. But the heavily favored Leafs pummeled the Bruins both on the scoreboard and on the ice, outscoring them 16–2 in taking the next four games. With two goals and two assists for four points and twenty-five minutes in penalties, Barilko had been a force for the Leafs. Even Bruins coach Lynn Patrick had been impressed.

"Barilko was just about their best man in the series," Patrick said.

Awaiting the Leafs now were their oldest rivals, the Canadiens, who'd beaten the juggernaut Wings despite finishing thirty-six points behind them in the standings. Richard had been the Canadiens' savior, delivering the team from sudden death twice at the hands of the Wings, first in the fourth overtime period of the opening game of the series and then in the third extra frame of the second game. Richard then added two more goals as the Canadiens closed out the series in six games.

The 1951 Stanley Cup Final brought together two teams moving in opposite directions. The Leafs were experienced and battle-tested, having won three of the previous four finals and five of nine. The Canadiens were younger and faster, led by a generation that would win the Cup six times over a run of ten straight appearances in the final. At the center of it all stood Barilko, tasked with holding the line between Toronto's past and Montreal's future.

What followed was a final for the ages.

Overtime in the Stanley Cup Final is a different country, governed by different laws, and played by different rules. Pressure breaks wills and blurs thought. Every player knows that one mistake can end everything, for better or worse. There is nothing else like it in professional team sports. In football, each team gets to possess the ball in overtime. In baseball, both teams get a turn at the plate in extra innings. In basketball and soccer, the game doesn't end with the first basket or successful strike but with the lapse of extra time. Only in hockey does the end come without expectation. There is no guaranteed equality of opportunity or potential reprieve from the gallows. Whether swift or delayed, the end is always sudden and never merciful.

The Leafs and Canadiens would deliver a master class in hockey's afterlife during the 1951 final. Five times they would take to the ice to contest the game's greatest prize, and five times the death knell would be sudden. Not once would the clock cue a celebration.

Game one set the bar for the series. Neither team gave an inch. From the opening face-off, the Leafs took it to the Canadiens, with Sid Smith scoring just fifteen seconds into the game. The Canadiens tied the game later in the period, when the Rocket intercepted Barilko's clearing attempt, deked around the startled defenseman, and beat Broda with a low hard shot to the corner.

"I tried to clear the puck, but Richard knocked it down," Barilko said. "I should've made sure I got it out of there."

Tod Sloan's goal just fifteen seconds later gave the Leafs back the lead and got Barilko off the hook, but Paul Masnick tied it for the Canadiens less than five minutes into the second period. Even though the Leafs badly outshot the Canadiens, thirty-nine to twenty-two, goaltender Gerry McNeil held the line to carry the Canadiens into overtime.

With the score tied 2–2, Barilko made up for his earlier mistake by saving a sure goal just a couple of minutes into overtime. After taking a pass from Elmer Lach, Richard looked to have Broda beat on a chance off the rush when Barilko suddenly appeared out of nowhere to deflect Richard's shot over the net and into the seats, denying the Rocket his second goal of the game. Soon after, Smith scored his second goal of the night to give the Leafs the win. But it was Barilko who was the talk of Toronto and the lead headline for his game-saving play in overtime:

BARILKO SAVED LEAFIAN BACON

"We wouldn't be feeling so good right now if it hadn't been for Barilko," Smythe said after the game. "That was really the old college try."

The Leafs had drawn first blood in the series, but the Canadiens had served notice that they weren't going down without a fight. It wasn't a blowout, it was a statement, by both teams, and a harbinger of things to come.

Through seven regular season games and one playoff game in Toronto, the Canadiens hadn't won all season at Maple Leaf Gardens. Not wanting to go back to Montreal down two, they responded with speed and urgency in the second game. They dominated the first half of the game, scoring a pair of goals to take a 2–0 lead. The Leafs answered back with a power-play goal late in the second period and then another approaching the midpoint of the third to tie the game 2–2.

After sixty minutes of regulation, the teams went back to overtime. This time, Barilko couldn't deny Richard his due. He could only watch helplessly from the bench as Doug Harvey took advantage of a lackluster Leafs line change that left Richard all alone at the Leafs' blue line. Harvey put a tape-to-tape pass onto the stick of the Rocket that sent him in alone on a mini breakaway. With a half-step on Mortson, Richard pulled away from the Leafs' defenseman, deftly drew Broda out of his net, deked around him cleanly, and then calmly put the puck into the vacated net for the winning goal. It was Richard's sixth of the playoffs and third winner in overtime.

The Leafs had thrown thirty-six shots at McNeil, to the Canadiens' twenty-four at Broda, but couldn't get more than two goals past the diminutive five-foot-seven goalie, who was turning in a postseason performance for the ages. The Canadiens had evened the series. After the game, they could be heard in the visitors' dressing room heartily singing the French folk song "Alouette." Had Barilko not saved the win for the Leafs in the first game, the Canadiens would've returned to Montreal up two games to none with a chance to sweep the series at home.

As the series shifted to Montreal, Primeau put Rollins back in goal for the first time since the opening game of the playoffs against the Bruins. Inspired by their home fans, the Canadiens came out flying, peppering Rollins with shots from every angle. The teams traded power-play goals by Richard and Smith but could muster no more past either Rollins or McNeil. For the third straight game, the teams would go to overtime.

It looked like Barilko might be the goat of the game when Richard deked around him to set up a point-blank shot on Rollins, but the Leafs' young netminder bailed out his defenseman with an acrobatic save. Seconds later, Ted Kennedy broke the hearts of the hometown fans not even five minutes into overtime when Sloan picked off an errant pass in the Canadiens' zone and fed it to the captain, who blasted a low, sharp-angle shot past McNeil for a 2–1 win. The Leafs had reclaimed the series lead, outshooting the Canadiens again, this time thirty to twenty-four. It was the only game of the series that wouldn't end 3–2.

By now, the press was already calling the 1951 final the "Overtime Series." Game four would bring more of the same. The Leafs jumped out to an early lead thanks to another quick strike by Smith, this time just thirty-eight seconds into the game. Knowing they couldn't afford to fall two games behind the Leafs going back to Toronto, the Canadiens played with desperation. Richard answered back later in the period to tie the game. Then after Howie Meeker put the Leafs ahead again early in the second period, Lach evened up the score again, tipping in a blast by Richard with just over six minutes to play in the third period.

For the first time in the series, the Canadiens had outshot the Leafs, twenty-one to nineteen. But fans would leave the Forum heartbroken once again. This time, it was Harry Watson for the win. In overtime, with the score tied 2–2, Watson jumped off the bench and immediately took a pass from Max Bentley then wired a twenty-foot shot past McNeil. Just one win away from the Stanley Cup, the Leafs had taken a stranglehold on the series heading back to Toronto.

On Saturday, April 21, 1951, fans filed into Maple Leaf Gardens for game five. They came by car, taxi, streetcar, and on foot. Some 14,577 in all, they packed the Gardens to the rafters, filled every seat. The fans in standing room–only tabled no complaints. They were just glad to be there.

Before the game even began, multiple "Go, Leafs, Go!" chants circled the arena. In the crowd was Barilko's mother, who'd come down from Timmins for the game. She always brought her son luck whenever she saw him play.

"That my Billy!" she screamed and pointed to her son as he took to the ice with his teammates. "That my Billy!"

The game was played with the weight of the Stanley Cup hanging in the air, under an electric tension that seemed to vibrate through the Gardens. The Leafs were determined and destined, the Canadiens desperate and dangerous. If the Leafs failed to win, they would have to try to close out the series in Montreal, where, although wounded, the Canadiens could draw energy from their rabid fan base.

The game unfolded as a masterpiece of defensive hockey. Chances were scarce. Every mistake felt fatal, every hit lingered longer, every inch of ice was contested. Barilko played one of the finest games of his career, taking a couple of penalties, leading several rushes, and nearly scoring on McNeil in regulation on a slap shot through a screen. Determined to pound the Canadiens into submission, he targeted every opponent within collision radius, dishing out heavy hits on Richard, getting into a dustup with Tom Johnson, and even engaging in a stick-swinging duel with McNeil.

The game itself was as closely contested as the first four. It was scoreless after the first period, which saw two players carried off on stretchers: Leafs captain Kennedy with a back injury (he would return) and Canadiens defenseman Bob Dawes with a gruesome, badly broken right leg (he would not, and never play again in the NHL). The irrepressible Richard broke through on a solo rush midway through the second period, picking up a pass at center ice, slicing through the Leafs' defense, and potting a backhand past Rollins to open the scoring. Just over three minutes later, though, Sloan tied it for the Leafs, fending off Harvey to beat McNeil.

Paul Meger put the Canadiens up 2–1 with a goal early in the third period. The Leafs pushed hard for the equalizer but kept getting turned away, as McNeil rejected Meeker, Kennedy, and Timgren in successive assaults.

With a face-off in the Canadiens' zone and his team down a goal with under a minute to play in the third period, Primeau pulled Rollins for an extra attacker. On the ice for the Leafs were future Hall of Famers Kennedy, Watson, and Bentley, along with Sloan, Mortson, and Smith. From his perch on the bench, Barilko watched nervously as Kennedy won the draw back to Bentley, who deftly deked around three Canadiens players and then drove to the slot for a shot. Bodies were everywhere in front of the Canadiens' crease. Bentley's shot struck a leg and then deflected off the post. But the home crowd had no time to lament the near miss. Sloan quickly corralled the loose puck and deposited it into the gaping net behind McNeil for his second goal of the game.

The clock showed thirty-two seconds left. The Leafs had tied the game.

Barilko and the rest of the Leafs' bench went ballistic. The crowd, dressed in their Saturday night best, erupted in a deafening roar. Maple Leaf Gardens shook to its foundation. The first four games had all gone into overtime, and now here it was upon them again, for a fifth straight game, a streak that'd never happened before in the final and hasn't happened since.

As the teams returned to their dressing rooms to contemplate the stakes before them, the crowd never let up in its demands.

"We want the Cup! We want the Cup! We want the Cup!" they chanted throughout the entire intermission.

The teams returned to the ice in opposite states of mind. While the Leafs, with the Stanley Cup within reach, practically leaped through the gates onto the ice, the Canadiens, with their Cinderella postseason one shot from ending, walked out of the visiting team's tunnel with their heads down and gingerly stepped onto the ice. Buoyed by Sloan's last-minute heroics, the Gardens' faithful were ready to explode.

Right from puck-drop, the Leafs pressed for the game-winning, series-ending, Stanley Cup–clinching goal in front of their home fans. In the Canadiens' net, McNeil turned away chance after chance and shot after shot as the Leafs came at him in wave after wave of attack.

Then, just over two minutes into extra time, Watson advanced the Leafs into the Canadiens' zone. Johnson rode him out in the corner, but

Watson was able to collect the puck and make a cross-ice pass to Meeker as he streaked toward the Canadiens' net down the right wing. Had he handled the pass cleanly, Meeker would've been the one to author the greatest moment in franchise history. Instead, he bobbled the puck, and his momentum forced him to go the long way around the net, passing teammate Cal Gardner as he sped to the other side. McNeil calculated Meeker's trajectory and met him at the opposite post just in time to foil his attempt for a wraparound goal. But in thwarting Meeker, McNeil stumbled and flopped helplessly onto his backside.

With the play continuing feverishly around him and the puck bouncing around the Canadiens' zone, McNeil hesitated between trying to get back to his feet, which would leave him momentarily unable to make a save, and being ready to stop a shot sitting down if one suddenly came his way. As McNeil floundered, Meeker managed to backhand the puck out to Watson, who'd moved into the slot, just as Johnson pinned Meeker face-first against the glass behind the net. Had his shot found the wide-open net, it would've actually been Watson who scored the greatest goal in Leafs history. Instead, it deflected off Butch Bouchard and drifted out to the face-off circle.

From there, the play developed innocuously. A scramble, a loose puck, chaos in front of the Canadiens' net. From his spot at the left point, Barilko watched it all unfold and reacted instinctively as the puck sprang loose to the right of McNeil. He left his position at the blue line, skated into the fray, lunged, and dove forward.

"Like Dagwood catching a bus," Smythe said.

The Goal

As coach, I had a couple of worries. One was stopping the great Rocket Richard, who had beaten us on a breakaway to win the second game for Montreal. My other concern was taming my aggressive defenseman, Bill Barilko. I had been after him for getting caught in the slot. For a defenseman to get caught up ice was poison. That was especially so against Richard, who would break out and be gone.

—Joe Primeau, Toronto Maple Leafs coach

SEVENTY-FIVE YEARS AFTER Bill Barilko made his desperate dive for the puck, there is no one left from his story. Family, friends, teammates, opponents, they're all gone. Whatever is left of it is archived in newspaper accounts of the period, and in the living memories of fans like Bill Hunter, the lucky ones who were there to witness it and are still with us.

Bill greets me at the entrance of The Village of Taunton Mills retirement home in Whitby, Ontario, and leads me up to his second-floor apartment, where he's lived for the past five years. A retired economics professor, he looks every bit professorial in a moss-green sweater overtop a light-green collared shirt, with greenish-brown slacks, brown shoes, glasses, and his neatly combed white hair.

Bill's apartment is clean and tidy. We sit down at the kitchen table, and he hands me a black-and-white photograph of Barilko. In it, Barilko, helmetless and hair coiffed, is holding his stick casually across his waist and looking down at his black-taped blade, willing it to do his bidding.

Bill took the photo at ice level during warm-ups from one of the many games his father took him to as a kid at Maple Leaf Gardens. Years later, Bill would be in the stands at the Gardens for three of four Stanley Cup–clinching games in the 1960s, missing only the Maple Leafs beating the Black Hawks in Chicago in 1962. But the conclusion to the 1951 showdown between the Toronto Maple Leafs and the Montreal Canadiens was his first and most memorable final.

"I've seen an awful lot of hockey games and had very good seats," Bill says. "But it's the one that's the clearest in my memory, and I think that's a function of the fact that I was young and it was a big deal for me."

Bill had just turned fourteen years old that day. His father had gotten him a ticket to the game for his birthday, with a seat about halfway up the corner blues. His dad didn't accompany him to the game, so Bill jumped on the Yonge Street streetcar solo (this was pre-subway) and made the trek down to Carlton Street.

"I got there and found my seat, and there were two quite vociferous French-Canadian men beside me," Bill says. "I don't know how much fuel they had, but they were pretty outspoken, so I just kept my head down because I was just a young kid."

Maurice Richard had given the two Canadiens fans plenty to cheer about when he opened the scoring midway through the second period, sweeping around Jimmy Thomson, deking Rollins out of his net, and then finishing the rush off with a low, hard backhand drive. It was his ninth goal of the playoffs.

In the illustrious career of the Rocket, his performance in the 1951 Stanley Cup playoffs, particularly the final, stands as his greatest individual postseason achievement, with nine goals, including three overtime winners. He'd scored twelve goals in the 1944 playoffs, but he was only a rookie then, a pure goal scorer with little responsibility on a veteran Canadiens team that ran away from the rest of the NHL by twenty-five points, losing only five times during the regular season and just once in the playoffs on their way to winning the Stanley Cup. Late in his career, he would come close to topping his rookie total, with eleven goals in the 1958 playoffs. But that was when Richard was part of the greatest dynasty in NHL history, with the likes of Dickie Moore, Jean Béliveau, Jacques Plante, and younger brother Henri Richard, as the Canadiens finished the season nineteen points clear of the rest of the league and were in the midst of winning the Stanley Cup five years in a row.

In 1951, Richard was in his prime, the Canadiens' leading scorer, the face of the franchise, and the only true superstar on a below-average team destined for greatness but whose time had not yet come. He'd single-handedly carried the Canadiens into the playoffs by just four points. Once there, he willed them into a monumental upset over the first-place Detroit Red Wings, who'd finished a full thirty-six points ahead of them. In six games, Richard scored four goals, including those two overtime winners on the road in Detroit. He then turned his fierce, fiery eyes upon the Maple Leafs in the Stanley Cup Final.

From his perch on the Leafs' bench, coach Joe Primeau could only stand and watch as Richard scored in every game of the series. All of them were big goals: two gave the Canadiens the lead, two tied the score, and the other won the game.

Game after game, Primeau looked on helplessly as Richard shook off every Leaf who attempted to defend him. The coach considered designating someone to shadow the Rocket, but that would've effectively taken one of his players out of the play whenever Richard was on the ice, which was more than a third of the game. Instead, Primeau had to trust his players to defend against Richard as a five-man unit and put his faith in Al Rollins to shoot down the Rocket whenever they failed.

For the Leafs' defensemen, that meant exercising exceeding caution whenever Richard was on the ice. As a left-handed shooter playing right wing, Richard would often come charging down the right side of the ice. As a right-handed shooter playing left defense, rare then and unheard of in today's NHL, Barilko would often be the one facing him. Never one to back down from a challenge, Barilko took aim at Richard at every opportunity. When he hit him, he hit him hard. When he missed, he missed badly.

Aggression was both Barilko's greatest weapon and weakness. When used right, he was relentless, punishing opponents with unstoppable checking and pursuing the puck with dogged determination. When used wrong, he was reckless, taking himself out of the play by overshooting his checks and chasing the puck with desperation. He was high-risk, which is why the Leafs sent him to Hollywood for polishing before they would even consider bringing him up to Toronto. He was also high-reward, which is why Conn Smythe saw something in Barilko that he believed would make him the quintessential Maple Leaf.

For the better part of the 1950–51 season, Primeau had worked hard at getting Barilko to control the aggression within. To harness it, to shape it, to use it only when necessary. It was a difficult task. Primeau even went so far as fining Barilko for disobeying a direct order. But Barilko's default was always to play at full throttle. He knew no other gear. To play halfway was to play half-assed, to decline his duty, to let down his teammates, and to cheat the game.

So, before the series against the Canadiens had even begun, Primeau pulled his overeager defenseman aside and told him in no uncertain terms never to pinch in from his post on the blue line in the offensive zone whenever Richard was on the ice.

"Bill, if you get caught up there," Primeau said to Barilko, "I'm going to fine you five hundred dollars, and five hundred dollars for every time after that."

For Barilko, who was making \$9,000 that season, \$500 was no small sum. So throughout the final, Barilko managed to rein himself in over the first four games and through sixty minutes of regulation in the fifth. After posting four points and twenty-five penalty minutes against the Boston Bruins in the semifinals, Barilko had done nothing offensively against the Canadiens, with zero points. He'd also kept his usual rambunctious, and occasionally reckless, self in check, earning only three minor penalties. But two of those had come in game five ahead of overtime. So, in the dressing room during the intermission, Primeau reminded Barilko of his explicit instructions and the monetary repercussions for disobeying them.

In hockey, however, decisions are made in milliseconds. They are reactions, not intentions. Eventually, instinct always takes over.

Young Bill Hunter watched from his prime perch in a corner of the blues behind the Canadiens' net as the Leafs stormed the offensive zone in overtime.

"After Tod Sloan, or 'Slinker' as he was known, had tied it up with about half a minute to go, when we came back after the intermission, the Frenchmen weren't there," Bill says. "I don't know what happened to them, but they must've lost faith. That was a relief to me because

I could cheer as much as I wanted, and I can remember the goal very clearly."

As the puck pinballed around the net, Bill edged farther and farther toward the end of his seat, until he was standing in heightened anticipation with the rest of the crowd. He watched the puck drift out to the face-off circle. At that moment, Barilko had a decision to make: hang back to guard against a counterattack by Richard, who was circling like a shark in the right corner, or abandon his post at the offensive blue line and try to get to the puck before any of the Canadiens, including the Rocket. With Richard on the ice, Barilko knew that Primeau would've wanted him to pull back, as he'd done all series long. Perhaps it was the taste of blood from a broken nose he'd sustained in the third period in a collision with Bert Olmstead that tapped into the primal part of Barilko. But as the chaotic play unraveled, Barilko smelled blood himself and began to sneak in surreptitiously from his spot at the left point, unbeknownst to everyone, even Foster Hewitt calling the game up in the Gardens' gondola. As he watched the puck bounce around the Canadiens' net, with Gerry McNeil flopping around on his backside, Tom Johnson pinning Howie Meeker behind the net, Butch Bouchard guarding Harry Watson in front of the net, and Richard in the right corner waiting for a chance at a counterattack, Barilko saw his destiny drift out to him.

From his seat in the crowd, no more than ten rows up from ice level, Bill watched as Barilko left his post, against his coach's instructions, as the puck popped out from the slot.

"I remember Barilko charging in from the left side on the blue line as the puck slid slowly out into the face-off circle," Bill says.

At 11:07 p.m. on April 21, 1951, at 2:53 of overtime, photographers Nat Turofsky and Michael Burns clicked their shutters, immortalizing the moment from opposite sides of the rink. In Turofsky's photograph, referee

Bill Chadwick has yet to signal a goal, the goal judge has yet to turn on the red light, the puck has yet to drop to the ice in the net, the Leafs have yet to celebrate, the Canadiens have yet to realize their heartbreak, and the crowd has yet to cheer. McNeil sits planted firmly on his Canadiens keister, eyes wide shut, his blocker raised in a desperate attempt to stop a shot he hasn't seen. Johnson presses Meeker's face into the boards behind the net, while Bouchard looks on helplessly from the slot with Watson, and Richard waits for a breakout pass he'll never receive. The Leafs' Cal Gardner looks over his right shoulder as he glides away from the play and into the corner to cover the Rocket.

Then there is Barilko, frozen in time, suspended in the air, yet to touch down, identifiable only by the number 5 on his sweater as the puck flies over the right shoulder of McNeil and kisses the net behind him. Of the five Leafs skaters on the ice, the only one not in Turofsky's photo is Barilko's defense partner, Fern Flaman, who'd held back at the blue line in case the Canadiens suddenly came the other way. Had Barilko flubbed his diving shot, Richard would've led an odd-man rush up ice for the Canadiens, with four Leafs, a sprawling and out-of-position Barilko among them, trapped in their end.

But Barilko didn't miss. In Burns' photograph, taken from the opposite side of the ice mere milliseconds after Turofsky's, Barilko is craning his neck as he watches the puck float past McNeil, who's looking behind him at the puck in the net and beginning to register the devastation of defeat.

The Gardens, including the young birthday boy in the corner blues, erupted.

"I was so excited and thinking how lucky I was and that it was my birthday," Bill recalls. "What a wonderful present."

With the two Canadiens fans beside him long gone, Bill cheered without restraint as Barilko jumped up off the ice and threw his arms into the air.

McNeil sat on the ice, stunned. The Canadiens players stood frozen in place, still processing what'd happened and unsure what to do next.

Meeker, who hadn't seen Barilko score, freed himself from Johnson's iron grip against the boards and was about to carve the big defenseman's head off with his stick when he saw that the red light was on.

"You big prick," Meeker said to Johnson as he turned to join the celebration. "The fucking thing is in the net. You lose."

The Leafs swarmed around Barilko, while teammates on the bench poured onto the ice and rushed toward him, as did his coach.

"Well, skipper," Barilko said to Primeau, "you didn't want the hook on me that time, did you?"

In the crowd, Barilko's mother had shut her eyes at the start of overtime and kept them closed until the cacophonous roar of the crowd forced them open.

"Is it over yet?" she asked the man beside her.

It was. Game over, series over. Her son had just scored the Stanley Cup–winning goal in overtime.

"That my son!" she screamed. "That my son!"

On the ice, Gardner and Bill Juzda lifted Barilko onto their shoulders. In an unchoreographed ceremony, NHL president Clarence Campbell presented the Stanley Cup to the Leafs, after which captain Kennedy and coach Primeau both spoke to the crowd. The Canadiens stayed long enough to shake hands with the victors, while the Leafs, to the roar of their fans, eventually retired to their dressing room. There were three cheers for Barilko, during which Rollins came over to him and planted a kiss on the forehead and a slap on the back as Barilko, with a beer in his left hand, punched the air above him with his right arm in celebration with his chanting teammates. Immortalized in Toronto but raised in Timmins, Barilko couldn't help but think of where it all started for him.

"Boy, wait until they find out about this back home," he said. "I'll be a real hero."

Barilko didn't need to tell them. All of Timmins had been listening, including his sister, Anne, as had his brother, Alex, who was in Sherbrooke, Quebec, at the time and quickly dispatched a telegram to Toronto in the wee hours of the morning after the game:

> *Congratulations on win tonight scoring the winner. Wish I had been there. Was listening and will never forget it. Give best to Mom and hope you have good time and rest. You deserve it. Don't forget what you want in contract for next season. Pay me a visit home in fall. Alex Barilko.*

In Maple Leaf Gardens, men became boys again, in both dressing rooms. As the Leafs whooped about, the Canadiens sat motionless. Reporters went into the visitors' room to find all the players sitting in their stalls, still fully dressed, staring into space. Richard wept, while coach Dick Irvin, usually sharp-tongued with intruding reporters, simply stared at the opposite wall. They had a right to be heartbroken but not regretful. Although they'd lost the series four games to one, and been badly outshot by the Leafs yet again, this time forty-one to nineteen, they'd just played the most tightly contested Stanley Cup Final in NHL history, with all five games going to overtime. Out of the 321 minutes and 41 seconds the two teams played, the games were either tied or separated by just one goal more than ninety-eight percent of the time. Only the Canadiens ever held a two-goal lead, and even then for only six minutes and six seconds.

When the printing presses began rolling, headlines in newspapers across Canada heralded the hero who'd returned the league's first dynasty to championship glory:

LEAFS WIN STANLEY CUP ON BARILKO OVERTIME GOAL

BARILKO SCORES IN OVERTIME, MAPLE LEAFS TAKE FINAL 3–2

BASHIN' BILL BARILKO'S BLOW KILLS CANADIENS

"That goal was a long time coming for me," Barilko said after the game. "But it sure was worth waiting for."

That night, fourteen-year-old Bill Hunter left the arena with 14,576 other witnesses to the greatest moment in Leafs history, while twenty-four-year-old Bill Barilko left the ice forever as a Stanley Cup champion for the fourth time in five years. Barilko was young, confident, and entering what promised to be the prime of his career, a defenseman at the peak of his powers skating toward future membership in the Hockey Hall of Fame.

The Fishing Trip

For those who care to take the leap, there is another way of remembering Bill Barilko, confined not by celebrity or by the tiny cockpit of a fragile yellow plane, a way of remembering him on the splendid last weekend of his life: Fishing.
—Charles Wilkins, "A Kid with a Smile and a Fishing Pole"

PORCUPINE LAKE LIES UNDER the Northern Ontario sky like a sheet of hammered steel. It spreads before me in a dull silver expanse, ringed by low houses with weathered docks. Behind me, a beaming Bill Barilko, his old Toronto Maple Leafs sweater bright in the morning light, greets those heading west into Timmins along Highway 101 and sends a glory-filled goodbye for those leaving it eastward.

From his billboard across the street, Barilko smiles toward the water. He sits there, half guardian and half ghost, looking over the lake he left behind and never returned to. His face is frozen forever at twenty-four, while the rest of us inch toward oblivion, gaining ever-deepening wrinkles and failing follicles. That is what's kept his story alive. Barilko never had the chance to become ordinary or old or play out his career into decline. Players don't leave the game, the game leaves them. But not Barilko. He left at his peak. For that, he remains preserved between victory and disappearance, the two fused together at the summit of his short life so completely that one can't be spoken of without the other.

Somewhere out across the water, some seventy-five years ago, a little floatplane lifted from the lake, its engine buzzing against the stillness, carrying Barilko north. Beside him was his dentist, Dr. Henry Hudson, piloting the plane, equally doomed and now largely overshadowed by hockey history. Two men lost in the wilderness, but only one is remembered, because he wore a Maple Leafs sweater and scored a goal that still resonates through generations. I picture the shoreline shrinking behind them and imagine the relief at escaping Barilko must've felt. There were no crowds, no reporters, no spotlight from Toronto following him into the wilderness. It was just him and his friend heading north of the Canadian Shield to where the rivers ran clear and cold and the fish waited.

Porcupine Lake is where the journey began. The shoreline is the last visible threshold between life and legend. Every mythic journey requires stepping through a doorway. Barilko's is Porcupine Lake.

In late August 1951, the dawn of another NHL season was still weeks away. Barilko had enjoyed his summer of celebrity, with people congratulating the overtime hero just about daily. But he longed for something he'd savored every summer since he was a kid: the promise of fish biting in quiet places.

That summer, Hudson planned a fishing trip, far north, up to Quebec's Seal River with his brother, Lou, who was also a dentist, and his friend Archie Chenier, who'd accompanied Hudson on several such trips before. This remote ribbon of water in Canada's Subarctic reaches salt water where James Bay and Hudson Bay meet, part of a vast, sparsely populated region where travel is by river, not road, and silence comes easily. He was an avid angler who knew the North not as a map of towns and highways but as a latticework of lakes and rivers. Hudson had made similar excursions many times before, flying into remote areas reachable only by his yellow Fairchild 24 bush plane.

Chenier, who built cottages and chalets, had to cancel last-minute when he landed a large contract.

"Henry, I can't go," he told his fishing buddy. "I've got to work."

Allan Stanley, a close friend of Barilko's and a fellow Timmins native who was playing with the New York Rangers at the time, was next in line but had to bow out too. Barilko, who'd been fishing longer than he'd been playing hockey, was a natural fit to take their place. Like the secondhand skates that got him into the game, Barilko's first fishing equipment was seconded to him out of miners' hand-me-downs. It consisted of a small gray childhood tackle box, with a stick and string for a fishing pole. He'd long graduated to a more sophisticated pole and line, as well as every manner of lure, but the same tackle box went with him wherever he fished, whether lakes like Temagami, Mattagami, or Watabeag south of Timmins, or now Seal River.

Although fishing had been an annual summer ritual for Barilko, since he was a boy, he'd never gone on a fly-in fishing trip before, never caught anything bigger or more exotic than perch, pike, or pickerel. He'd never dropped a line in a body of water so remote, never fished in a place where time stood still and the landscape hadn't changed since the last glacier had sculpted it into form thousands of years earlier.

The plan was simple. Hudson would fly them 644 kilometers (400 miles) north to Seal River in his single-engine, float-equipped bush plane. It was a route he'd flown several times before. The two men would depart on the last Friday of August from Hudson's dock on Porcupine Lake, east of Timmins. They would stop to refuel in the small community of Rupert House and then carry on to Seal River. Once on its banks, the two of them would spend a couple of days fishing for Arctic char and then return home Sunday night in plenty of time for Barilko to drive back to Toronto the following day ahead of training camp in St. Catharines. He'd have a tale guaranteed to trump every one of his teammates' summer fishing stories.

The morning of their departure, Friday, August 24, Barilko quietly opened the door to his mother's bedroom to say goodbye. For the first time in her life, she didn't stir. She didn't turn around to say goodbye or kiss him farewell. When he'd told her about the trip earlier in the week, she was angry about the chosen day of his departure. Her husband had died on a Friday five years earlier, and she never wanted any of her three children to take a risk on that one day of the week. In her broken English, she'd pleaded with him not to go, not that far, not on that day.

"Billy, don't go," she'd said. "Please, no go fishing. Not on Friday. I no like Friday."

That her son was planning to fly into bush country he'd never been to and had no experience of only made her madder. So, when his mother didn't say goodbye, Barilko was sad but not surprised. As he closed the door quietly, he carried a piece of his mother's sorrow with him. He then grabbed the lunch his sister, Anne, had made for him, because his mother refused to do so, and left for Porcupine Lake.

At Hudson's dock, the plane bobbed near the shoreline like some restless northern bird. It was a familiar sight to fourteen-year-old Gaetan Lepine, whose family lived next door to the Hudsons. The evening before the fishing trip, Hudson's wife, Phyllis, had leaned across the fence and told him that her husband would be flying out in the morning with Bill

Barilko. She suggested that Lepine come over early, before dawn had fully lifted, and her husband would introduce them. Perhaps she didn't know that the boy was a die-hard Montreal Canadiens fan.

The next morning, mist hovered low over the water as Lepine crossed the yard toward the dock, his stomach tight with nerves. By then, Hudson and Barilko were already busy loading the plane. Bill Curik had driven Barilko to Hudson's place to see his friend off. Piece by piece, Hudson and Barilko packed the plane with the patience of men heading far into the wilderness. Rods and tackle boxes disappeared into the cargo space beside rolled sleeping bags, canvas tents, crates of supplies, and heavy tins of food, chiefly for Barilko, who detested the taste of fish.

Barilko looked larger in person than Lepine had imagined from newspaper photographs. Broad-shouldered and quiet, Barilko wasn't glamorous in the way hockey heroes seemed in print and over radio. He moved with an easy confidence that made the dock feel smaller around him.

When Hudson introduced them, Lepine shook Barilko's hand and immediately forgot everything he'd planned to say. Words tangled in his throat. He stared down at the dock, blushing furiously.

"You beat my Canadiens," he managed to squeak out at last.

Barilko smiled faintly, almost apologetically.

"It was a tough game," he said so as not to deepen the injury he'd unknowingly dealt the boy.

For a few minutes, Lepine helped the men finish loading the plane, handing over bags and boxes while the lake lapped softly against the floats below them. Then, with the work done, he drifted back across the yard toward home, glancing once over his shoulder at Barilko beside the aircraft. He'd come expecting to dislike the player who'd beaten his Canadiens. Instead, he left thinking Barilko seemed like a good man.

With Hudson that morning was his older brother, Lou, who was supposed to come along too. But so heavily laden was the plane that, in the absence of a strong wind, it couldn't develop enough lift to get off the water and above the trees into the mid-morning sky. The three of them tried taking off using the slipstream of another pilot, but the Fairchild was just too heavy. Someone had to stay behind. Since Lou had already joined his brother on trips like this before, he let Barilko go instead.

As Barilko reboarded the plane, he turned to Curik, laughing, and slapped his longtime friend on the shoulder.

"If I don't come back," he told him, "be sure to send me some daisies."

As the plane lifted up off the lake and turned north, the gridwork of farms and roads gave way to irregular shapes as they flew into the heart of the Hudson Plain. Below them were dark bands of spruce, rivers threading through the muskeg, and lakes like spilled mercury. From the air, the land looked endless and untouched, an impression that only deepened as their flight continued.

Three hours and 380 kilometers (236 miles) later, the plane touched down on the water at the edge of Rupert House. As they taxied into the dock, Hudson and Barilko were met by James Crawford, an eighteen-year-old Toronto transplant who'd just gotten a job with the Hudson's Bay Company fur department a few months earlier. Crawford wasn't a hockey fan, so he didn't recognize Barilko. Instead of talking hockey, they talked fishing. Crawford had heard of Seal River but hadn't been there yet. Even though he hadn't yet fished there himself, Hudson knew the bounty of Arctic char that awaited them within the river's waters. Seeing Crawford's eyes light up at the prospect, Barilko promised him one of their haul's on their way back two days hence.

Hudson and Barilko carried on to Seal River, arriving there that Friday. Older and more experienced in these trips, Hudson took the lead in logistics, setting up the tent, storing the supplies, and keeping an eye on conditions. Barilko, younger and stronger, was eager to help wherever he could without getting in the way.

The two men needed no guide. All they had to do was get to the river, and the fish would do the rest. Every year, hundreds of thousands of mature Arctic char return to Seal River upstream from Hudson Bay and the northern part of James Bay. They come back to spawn in the shallow, stony headwaters where they hatched, releasing and fertilizing their eggs in the cold running water in an unceasing cycle of life. Come spring, the newly hatched inch-long fingerlings struggle upward through the gravel of the riverbed to feed and grow into six-inch adolescents. Then begins a quiet exodus into the open waters of Hudson Bay and James Bay. In those vast subarctic seas, the young fish mature until they're old enough to make the long journey to the river of their birth, where fishers like Hudson and Barilko welcome them home.

For two days, daylight dictated time rather than the pocket watch Hudson had bought in Switzerland the year before. Mornings began early, with mist lifting from the river and the fish feeding close to the surface. Like he did with his defense partners, Barilko found camaraderie with Hudson, despite their twenty-three-year age gap. Conversation, when it was warranted, flowed easily, breaking the long stretches of silence only when words were necessary. Without the distractions of urban life, and the press of professional responsibilities, small details bubbled to the surface: the sound of water against the shore, the sudden weight on a line, the smell of fish cooking over an open fire. Time slowed. Evenings were spent watching the light fade, the sky deepening in color as the sun set, and then turning into a black starry heavens that cities never see.

Although the wilds of Northern Quebec were foreign land to Barilko, he'd grown up in Northern Ontario, where the outdoors isn't a novelty but a fact of life. Lakes and forests were friendly terrain to him. He wasn't some pampered star athlete from the city slumming it in the bush. He was a hardy northern kid from a mining town venturing into a landscape he hadn't been to before but understood. He wasn't escaping hockey so much as balancing it. Although his public identity was synonymous with life on the blueline wearing the blue and white, privately he was a man of simple pleasures. For a defenseman whose professional life was built on aggression and assertiveness, the patience and humility that come with waiting until the fish decides to be caught was a soothing contrast. In a life shaped by train schedules and ever-increasing public attention, the river offered Barilko a return to his youth, and the fish a reminder of how much he missed it. Casting lines, cleaning fish, tending the fire, all the routines of fishing camp were familiar and reassuring, at odds with the intensity and competition of training camp, which beckoned upon his return.

There were no trophies for a successful catch, no records kept. Just the experience itself, in days lived slowly, deliberately, attentively. Barilko went north because he loved to fish, because he enjoyed the company and camaraderie, because the water was calling. For a brief stretch of summer, that was all he needed.

Disappearance

It seems unbelievable, one minute we were carrying him off the ice on our shoulders and the next minute he was gone.
—Bill Juzda, Toronto Maple Leafs teammate

FROM TIMMINS, I CROSS over into Quebec and carry on to Val-d'Or, where I stop for fuel. The clerk barely looks up. To him, I am just one more passing instance in a day made entirely of them. He doesn't know the route I'm retracing or the two destinations I'm revisiting. Even if he did, he wouldn't care why. He's probably a Montreal Canadiens fan anyway.

Beyond Val-d'Or, hours pass in that drifting, attentive way that only long drives allow. Unwilling to follow me farther north, the radio begins to lose conviction, as stations dissolve into static, leaving me without any hockey talk to listen to. When I reach the Billy-Diamond Highway, at the mining town of Mattagami, the road heads north with a kind of indifference, straight in places where I expect curves and curving only when it must. There are fewer vehicles now. Sometimes, none at all for long stretches. At one point, I step out and stand in the middle of the road to soak in the silence, until another vehicle appears in the distance, like a thought I didn't realize I was having.

At Relais Routier du Km 381, the only way station en route, I stop for the night. The fluorescent lighting inside this outpost at the edge of nowhere is strangely pleasant, and the greasy food and no-nonsense cooks are oddly comforting. People speak quietly or not at all. Everyone is passing through, and everyone knows it.

The next morning, on the final stretch north, the road, the trees, and the long, low horizon repeat until they begin to feel inevitable. At the highway's end, I take the last turnoff and arrive in Chisasibi an hour later. I drive through town to the edge of the mainland until the land begins to open toward the wide, slow breadth of James Bay.

For me, this isn't just landscape. It is aftermath.

On August 26, 1951, Bill Barilko came this way by air on his return from Seal River with Henry Hudson. Carrying more story than it knew, Hudson's small floatplane had turned south toward two Cree towns along the bay.

What I'm experiencing as a drive, they knew as approach.

They landed at the small island community of Fort George, about 161 kilometers (100 miles) due south of Seal River. The island seemed both fragile and precise, held in place by will more than the earth that was slowly eroding and would eventually force the community inland thirty years later, where it is now known by its Cree name, Chisasibi. As they made their descent, the engine dropped in pitch, the nose tilted toward the water, and the floats touched down with that brief, skidding hesitation before settling. Where they landed, the water was tinged orange from the fuel of all the planes flying in and out of the island.

At the short ferry crossing to Fort George, a piece of the Barilko legend finds me as I speak with the ferry operator. His father had told him that his grandfather had spoken with Hudson and Barilko on their fishing trip. Could his granddad have talked with them on their way to or from Seal River back in 1951? Like so much of the story, the details have been lost to time. People continue to inject themselves into the story, like those who claimed to have been the one Barilko replaced on the plane that fateful weekend, enough to fill a jetliner, not a small floatplane. None of it matters, though. It is no sin against the story if they do. It says something that, all these years later, people are still coming to the story, seeking out the legend, and trying to find their tiny place within it.

Weighed down by their bounty from a prolific weekend of fishing, Hudson had decided to make a quick pit stop on the small island to unload some of their camping gear at another Hudson's Bay Company trading post and have them hold it until he returned the following summer. They landed only long enough to refuel and mark the place in their logbook. Hudson chatted briefly with Reita Shepherd, wife of the local Anglican missionary. She invited them to stay for lunch, but Hudson had his dental practice to get back to, and Barilko had a send-off party to attend before leaving for training camp the next day.

"Thank you," Hudson told her. "But we have to get home for supper."

As Hudson unloaded their gear, Barilko chatted with Shepherd's two sons and offered them tickets to a game if they ever found their way to Toronto. He was happy and in high spirits after a weekend of fishing like no other. Within ten minutes, Hudson and Barilko were off again. It was just after one o'clock.

I leave Chisasibi and head back down the Billy-Diamond Highway, driving parallel to Hudson's line of flight. As I head south, the land tightens and loosens again, a rhythm of low forest and open wetland.

The sky feels closer. I begin to sense how a pilot might navigate up here by instinct instead of instruments, following the curve of the shoreline and the angle of light.

After stopping for the night again at Relais Routier du Km 381, I carry on the next day and drive to the edge of Rupert River, once a vital fur trade route for the Hudson's Bay Company and the Cree. From the air in 1951, the river would've looked like a threshold, its dark waters cutting through lighter marsh, the buildings gathered close to the shore, the suggestion of docks, of movement, of lives arranged around water. After another descent, another careful landing, floats kissing the surface, once again yet for the last time, the plane settled into the current's quiet insistence.

Three hours and 233 kilometers (145 miles) after leaving Fort George, Hudson and Barilko landed here, at what was then called Rupert House but has since also reverted to its Cree name, Waskaganish. This time, they were met by twenty-three-year-old Dan Wheeler, a clerk with the Hudson's Bay Company trading post in town. James Crawford wasn't working but had seen the Fairchild fly in, so he ran over to the dock to greet the men again and inquire as to their fishing trip. As he'd promised Crawford two days earlier, Barilko pulled out one of their dozens of fish and handed it to him and then gave three more to some Cree men down at the dock. As Wheeler refueled the plane, Eva Williams, wife of the local Anglican missionary, caught sight of Barilko from the hill above as he walked along the dock.

"You must like it up in this country," she shouted.

Barilko smiled widely. "I sure do."

It'd been a rough flight from Fort George. Hudson was clearly tired from battling strong headwinds that nearly halved the plane's usual cruising speed of 148 kilometers (92 miles) per hour. It was a muggy, humid day, and a storm was barreling in from the south, right in the Fairchild's flight path. Visibility was anywhere between 5 and 10 kilometers (3 and 6 miles), and the wind was coming from the southwest at about 24 to 29 kilometers (15 to 18 miles) per hour. But at two thousand feet, where Hudson and Barilko would be flying, it was much stronger, with the winds between 64 and 89 kilometers (40 and 55 miles) per hour. Crawford offered the men beds at the post. Wheeler also urged Hudson to wait out the storm and stay overnight. But Hudson told him not to worry, he was used to flying in such conditions. Besides, they had to get back to Timmins or the haul of fish they'd caught would all spoil.

Shortly after four o'clock, Hudson and Barilko piled into the plane again and taxied away from the dock. Thunder and lightning could be seen in the distance. It took Hudson several tries to get the plane off the water. When it finally did, half an hour later, it barely cleared the tree line east of town, and the plane rolled so violently from wingtip to wingtip that one woman thought the pilot was doing stunts. Hudson circled north, then came back over the post and hugged the shoreline until the plane passed out of sight, heading in a westerly direction. The plane had a full tank of gas with a safe endurance of four hours.

Having retraced the Fairchild's flight path, as much as the roads here allow, I head back home, passing stretches where the road runs arrow-straight. It is impossible not to look up. There is nothing there, of course. Only sky, ungraspable and unbroken. But knowing what once moved through it changes the way I see it. Fort George and Rupert House, now Chisasibi and Waskaganish, they are no longer just points on a map. They are the last confirmed accounts of a story that didn't end cleanly and, instead, has left us with myth and mystery.

On a clear day, it would've taken Hudson and Barilko about three hours to fly from Rupert House to Timmins. But with the gale-force headwinds they encountered, the cruising speed of the Fairchild would've been dramatically reduced to between 40 and 56 kilometers (25 and 35 miles) per hour. The plane held about fifty gallons of gas and burned roughly nine to eleven gallons per hour, giving them a range of 258 kilometers (160 miles), well short of the 380 kilometers (236 miles) to Timmins.

In Hudson's flight plan, his intention was to fly from Rupert House, via Kesagami Lake, to the South Porcupine Seaplane Base on Porcupine Lake. If he stuck to his course, they would've encountered headwinds from the southwest of nearly 93 kilometers (58 miles) per hour under a ceiling of just five hundred feet with a visibility of just half a mile and the potential for carburetor icing as they approached Kesagami Lake, about 241 kilometers (150 miles) northeast of Timmins. The winds were so strong that a pilot with Austin Airways flying in the opposite direction, with the aid of what for him were tailwinds, made the 338-kilometer (210-mile) trip from Timmins to Moosonee, on the southern edge of James Bay, in half the time it usually took.

Hudson could've tried to hold his course. Or, he had several options open to him if the storm forced him off his original flight path. He could've attempted to fly over it. He could've outflanked it by turning west for Moosonee, or landing on one of the many ponds and lakes in that part of the Hudson Plain, or by following the Ontario Northland Railway line south that ran between Moosonee and Cochrane. He could've also followed the Moose River south and then along the connected Mattagami River all the way down to Timmins.

When Hudson and Barilko didn't return home as planned Sunday night, those who were expecting them assumed they'd either stayed an extra day to fish or landed on one of the many lakes in the Hudson Plain to wait out the weather and perhaps even refuel using one of several caches that Hudson either owned or knew about. He'd done so before after encountering engine trouble on a previous trip a couple of years earlier. But when the two men didn't show up by Monday morning, four local pilots set out in search of them, starting with Kesagami Lake, where they thought Hudson was likely to have set down. When that turned up empty, they searched the small settlement west of the lake called Coral Rapids, where a hydro survey crew had seen a plane flying into strong headwinds on Sunday evening.

By Monday afternoon, the media had picked up the story. By Tuesday morning, it was front-page news:

> BARILKO VANISHES IN NORTH

From there, the search was officially on.

Knowing that the size of the search area would be well beyond what their resources could handle, the Ontario Provincial Police, in consultation with the Ontario Department of Lands and Forests, immediately alerted the Royal Canadian Air Force Rescue Coordination Centre in Trenton, Ontario, one of four such centers across Canada. While an advance search base was being set up in the town of Kapuskasing, about 121 kilometers (75 miles) northwest of Timmins, the RCAF dispatched two Dakota transports carrying pararescue crews to search for the men along their intended route. The air force also issued a telegram:

> *Indications are that additional aircraft will be required. Press Toronto very interested and want full coverage. Passenger Barilko is Toronto Maple Leaf star.*

Meanwhile, six private planes, one with Hudson's brother, Lou, aboard, set out to check any pond or lake where Hudson might've landed. Both searches had to be called off early when an electrical storm rolled in. Inspector Ike Robbie, who was leading the OPP's investigation of the missing men, cautioned against the probability of finding them there.

"There would be almost one hundred miles of dangerous bush country without lakes," he said, "which they would have to cross on their flight."

Word of the missing men had already reached their families by Monday morning. Barilko's sister, Anne, found out first. When her brother didn't turn up later that day, she reluctantly told their mother, who became hysterical at the news.

"Why Billy no come home?" she cried.

For her part, Phyllis Hudson wasn't worried. On a similar fishing trip two years earlier, her husband, flying alone, was forced down because of battery trouble and lived off the land for four days until he was found.

"As far as I'm concerned, they're not missing," she said. "They are out of gas and down on some lake. My husband is a very careful pilot, and bad weather or lack of gas may have forced him down."

Chenier, who was Hudson's most frequent fishing companion, would've disagreed with her assessment of her husband's judgment while in the air. Chenier survived several brushes with disaster alongside his close friend. On one trip, the plane ran out of gas just a few miles north of Cochrane. Only at Chenier's repeated insistence did Hudson set it down rather than try to stretch his glide and reach town.

"Let's put her down, Henry," Chenier told Hudson, who had a bad habit of flying low on fuel. When Hudson kept flying, Chenier had to repeat his plea. "Let's put her down, Henry."

On another trip, the two men set out for a flight north of Cochrane, lifting off from Porcupine Lake beneath a clear sky, only to wheel back moments later when Hudson realized he'd forgotten to fuel the aircraft.

It was the sort of oversight that might've been comical had it not carried such obvious consequences.

Another time, while drinking away a Sunday together in Temagami, Hudson was about to try to fly back to Timmins that night for work in the morning. Chenier managed to convince him to stay the night in town.

On yet another trip together, at Hudson's cottage on Lake Temagami, the men had gotten barely two hundred feet in the air after takeoff when the engine burst into flames. They were able to land safely and put the fire out, but the engine was so badly burned that Hudson had to buy a new one. The aircraft Hudson owned had actually been designed for wheels, not floats. The seaplane variant called for a more powerful engine, but he acquired the float gear anyway and had it installed despite knowing the plane would be underpowered. From that moment on, every departure from water became a calculated gamble. The aircraft depended on a strong headwind to lift itself from the surface, gathering speed reluctantly before clawing its way into the air. The strain told on the machine. The engine was pushed beyond what it'd been built to endure, burning fuel at an accelerated rate and developing a succession of mechanical troubles. Oil leaks became a recurring affliction, each repair offering only temporary relief before another seep appeared.

One such instance occurred on a return trip to Timmins together when oil began leaking from the engine, forcing Hudson and Chenier down onto a lonely lake near Cochrane. Fortune, thin as it was, placed a cottage on the shoreline and a road within reach. They managed to secure a ride into town and returned with oil, though aviation fuel was nowhere to be found. With little choice, they took off again. The aircraft, already underpowered, clawed its way above the black spruce, skimming the treetops as if reluctant to leave them behind. By the time they reached

Porcupine Lake, the fuel tanks were nearly dry, running on little more than hope and fumes. Chenier never flew with Hudson again.

Well south of the search for Hudson and Barilko, Louise Hastings stared out across the water on the shores of Lake Simcoe, about an hour north of Toronto, where her family had rented a cottage. The day before, she'd been waiting for Barilko to roll up in "Black Beauty," his Chevrolet, on his way to training camp in St. Catharines. When she heard the news on the radio, she went out and sat on the beach alone. The pair had been dating, and Hastings had even been up to Timmins to meet his family. With her birthday coming up on September 4, she'd been expecting Barilko to propose when he arrived. Her mother came up to her and hugged her tight, while her father, not usually one for showing affection, went over to his heartbroken daughter and gave her a hug and a kiss.

"Don't worry, they'll find him," he told her. "They'll find him."

On the first full day of the rescue mission, August 29, three days after Hudson and Barilko were supposed to have returned, the RCAF searched some 9,656 square kilometers (3,728 square miles) of the Hudson Plain, focusing on Hudson's intended flight path from Rupert House. Led by search master Flight Lieutenant G. J. "Rusty" Ruston, the search was officially called "Operation Hudson" but was more often dubbed "Operation Barilko" by both air force crews and the press. An expanded radio network included the Department of Lands and Forests, the Hudson's Bay Company, and Austin Airways. The search started with twenty military planes, including wartime Lancaster and Mitchell bombers as well as Dakotas, a Norseman, and a Canso flying boat, and involved more than a hundred crew members. Together, they began searching an area of 96 kilometers (60 miles) on either side of the plane's track line from Rupert House to the South Porcupine Seaplane Base. There was also a heavy police presence from the OPP, many of whom were helping out with the search but some of whom were doing a secret, potentially criminal, investigation of their own.

The RCAF had to cover tens of thousands of square miles of a desolate, largely uninhabited and unforgiving part of the country about the size of Texas. The Hudson Plain is made up of poorly drained terrain locked in permafrost and filled with muskeg, swampy bush, scrub timber, ponds, rivers, lakes, and islands. Canada is home to about one-quarter of the world's wetlands. Most of that is found in the Hudson Plain, which covers four percent of Canada and twenty-five percent of Ontario. In all, the RCAF would have to search some 369,000 square kilometers (142,472 square miles) of land and 11,800 square kilometers (4,556 square miles) of water.

"With as much territory as we have to cover," Ruston said, "that amounts to looking under every twig."

Meanwhile, fellow players from Timmins, including Allan Stanley and Bep Guidolin, who'd battled Barilko many times as a member of the Chicago Black Hawks, had gathered together at the local airport in town in hopes the men would be found soon.

"It will be a bad show if Bill gets his in a thing like this," Guidolin said.

In the early days of the rescue mission, the search was based on the hope that Hudson had either set the plane down safely on some lake or the two men had survived a crash. If they had, and the plane wasn't badly damaged, Hudson would've likely set a smudge fire on the pontoons as well as a fire in the bush, which could've been seen up to 24 kilometers (15 miles) away in clear visibility. Although the Fairchild had normal emergency equipment for the time, that didn't include an emergency locating transmitter nor a functioning radio. Hudson and

Barilko would've had to shelter in place and wait for help to arrive, as the Hudson Plain is passable only in winter when everything freezes. They had enough food to survive on, but they would've had to contend with hordes of blackflies and mosquitoes, which alone could've required hospitalization within two days.

"We're counting on the fact Dr. Hudson, the pilot, is an experienced pilot and knows the country well," Ruston said. "Both men are said to be able to take care of themselves in the bush."

With Barilko missing somewhere in the woods, locals old enough to remember couldn't help but recall a twenty-two-year-old man who went missing in the bush on a hunting trip outside Timmins back in 1937. His name, too, was Bill Barilko. He survived six days in the woods before he was found. Having a rifle but no ammunition, he stayed alive by killing two partridges with stones and a rabbit with a stick and also by finding some tea in an empty shack. Fourteen years later, the hope was that his twenty-four-year-old cousin would be as fortunate.

At the family home, Barilko's mother continued to hold out hope that her youngest son would return home safe and sound. Although she'd barely left her house since her husband died five years earlier, and had never flown in her life, she boarded a plane to Kapuskasing so that she could be as close to her son as possible, wherever he was. Alex joined his mother at Kapuskasing.

"I know because I watch him play, I bring luck to him," Barilko's mother told reporters. "When I near him, he have luck, always. This why I go very close to Bill, before they find him even."

From August 30 until September 5, rescue workers logged one hundred hours of combined flying time daily, covering more than 51,800 square kilometers (20,000 square miles). In all that week, they searched 567,599 square kilometers (219,152 square miles) during nearly seven hundred hours of flying time. Aerial assistance came from everywhere. Government agencies, commercial airlines, and private pilots all offered their services and aircraft in the search. Family and friends volunteered as spotters, everyone from Barilko's brother, Alex; to his brother-in-law, Emil Klisanich; friends Leo Curik and Allan Stanley; and Hudson's brother, Lou. Reporters did as well, though more so hoping to scoop the RCAF and find the men themselves. For the first week, newspapers, both local and national, provided daily updates. But as the search entered its second week, the daily reports began to dwindle and leave the front pages, drifting further and further back as the rescue effort dragged on.

For the first ten days, the weather largely cooperated with the search, with clear skies and good visibility, though below freezing temperatures at night led to hoarfrost on the aircraft, delaying morning departures. But a week into September, snow, rain, high winds, and low ceilings began to hinder the effort and even endanger aircraft and crews. One of the search planes skidded off the runway, while another lost power in one of its engines midflight at less than two thousand feet about 161 kilometers (100 miles) from Kapuskasing, as did a helicopter that crashed just off the shore of Rupert River. On the ground, two groups of searchers lost their way and had to be rescued. No lives were lost, but the combination of poor sleep, bad weather, a breakout of scarlet fever at a radio post in Rupert House, and even sightings of polar bears in the extended search area into northwestern Quebec were complicating an already complex mission. There were also unrelated reports of missing persons in eastern Manitoba, northwestern Quebec, and Georgian Bay, Ontario, each of which temporarily diverted RCAF planes from Operation Hudson.

More significantly, the grind of searching for the yellow Fairchild in the vast emptiness of the Hudson Plain was beginning to take its toll on the pilots and spotters. The search required intense concentration to scan mile after mile of the same monotonous landscape in what amounted to a "tree by tree" search, as Ruston put it. Between briefings, checks, preparation, and actual flying time, most of the crews were logging upward of fifteen-hour days. Time and again, a spotter would catch sight of a patch of yellow in the mass of muskeg and point and yell for the plane to circle around the area of interest, only to discover that it was nothing more than discolored leaves in the forest or a sandbar or beaver dam in the water. One of the Lancasters was later equipped with a camera to take aerial photographs of the search area so that air force photo evaluators could examine them under a microscope in hopes of finding something of the missing men that search crews hadn't seen.

"Although we've covered the whole territory, we're still quite optimistic," Ruston said. "Our survival experts have told us that if Barilko and Dr. Hudson are down without being too badly injured, they should be able to survive indefinitely in the bush in this weather."

As the search went from days to weeks, the planes began running short of fuel. Imperial Oil stepped in, shipping gasoline by both road and rail to keep the aircraft airborne. Kapuskasing was overwhelmed by RCAF staff and all the newspaper reporters scouring for scoops. Among the gaggle of reporters, most of whom were from Toronto, was Ben Ward, a staff reporter for the *North Bay Nugget.* For Ward, who joined RCAF crews in the air in the early days of the mission, the search was personal.

"Bill Barilko and I went through school together," he wrote. "This thing couldn't have happened to a nicer guy."

While the airborne search was underway, the RCAF and OPP filtered through dozens of reported sightings. There was a report that a small plane had crashed north of Cochrane, while a railway worker reported that a plane had descended rapidly into a forested area south of the town. Neither turned up anything. Nor did a report of a small plane experiencing engine trouble or running out of gas near the town of Matheson, east of Timmins. With no solid leads, the RCAF and the OPP had to investigate dozens of reports of sightings, crashes, smoke, fires, fabric, tents, canoes, fuel caches, and even an airplane window. One came from an Ontario Northland Railway clerk who reported seeing two flares, "lit like Roman candles," one night nearly three weeks into the search.

"So far as we have been able to determine, the missing Fairchild was not equipped with emergency flares," Ruston said. "Nevertheless, all reports have been closely checked by our aircraft."

By September 17, family and friends of the missing men had raised enough money, mostly through benefit softball games Turk Broda organized with NHL players, to post a $1,000 reward (about $12,000 seventy-five years later) leading to the whereabouts of Hudson and Barilko. By then, about three weeks into the search, the RCAF had already begun to reduce its commitment. A week later, it ceased operations altogether, though a Lancaster quietly continued searching the area and taking aerial photographs into mid-October.

When the Leafs arrived in St. Catharines on September 23 for their medical checkups ahead of training camp, many of the players hadn't seen Barilko since he'd scored his Stanley Cup–winning goal five months earlier. The team had already canceled a planned banquet to honor its 1951 championship.

"We're going to training camp this Sunday under sad conditions," said Conn Smythe. "Little hope is held out for the safety of Barilko."

Eight defensemen were listed on the training camp roster. Barilko was one of them. Perhaps Smythe just didn't have the right words to soften the obvious blow when he bluntly told reporters ahead of the opening day of camp, "Someone will have to take Bill's place if he doesn't show up."

Among the many hopefuls was twenty-one-year-old defenseman Tim Horton, who'd impressed management at camp the year before when he'd turned the tables on Barilko and Barilkoed him with a stiff bodycheck. Horton had spent the 1949–50 season in the American Hockey League with the Pittsburgh Hornets but got into one regular season game and one more in the playoffs with the Leafs. Reporters were already touting him as Barilko's likely replacement ahead of the 1951–52 season. But just as the Leafs had done with Barilko, shipping him south to Hollywood for more seasoning, they sent Horton back to Pittsburgh, where he would spend another season with the Hornets, winning the AHL championship in 1952 before finally cracking the Leafs' lineup for good in the 1952–53 season. Born in Cochrane, bred on the same values, built in the same mold, with the same height and weight, and shooting right-handed, it would be the hard-nosed Horton who would eventually take Barilko's spot, and replace his playing style, on the Leafs' defense corps.

At training camp, Gus Mortson, who was born in New Liskeard, Ontario, and had spent many years hunting and fishing in Northern Ontario, offered his own take on what might've happened to Barilko. If Hudson had been following the Canadian Pacific Railway line from James Bay to fly around the storm, he might've gotten mixed up and followed the Canadian National Railway line instead, which would've taken them east and forced him to ditch the plane in Lake Abitibi, a large lake east of Cochrane that straddles the border between Ontario and Quebec.

"It's a shallow lake and very rough most of the time," Mortson said. "I figure they might have landed on it when the gasoline ran out and that the plane might have sunk and they managed to swim to one of the islands. It's just a hunch, but I haven't seen anything said of a search being made around that lake and I think it well worthwhile."

Like every other theory, lead, and clue, nothing turned up at Lake Abitibi.

On September 25, nearly one month after Hudson and Barilko had disappeared, and no closer to knowing their whereabouts than when they'd started, the RCAF called off the search. Over thirty days, far longer than the ten days the air force usually allotted for a search and rescue mission, at a cost of somewhere between $385,000 and $500,000 (about $5 million to $6 million seventy-five years later), Operation Hudson had covered 843,505 square kilometers (325,679 square miles) using 38 RCAF planes that spent 1,354 hours aloft. Two hundred and seventy RCAF personnel, from pilots and navigators in the air to radio operators and ground crews on land, had been involved. The search was so thorough and concentrated that the air force found two other missing plane wrecks: a Seabee from 1948 just north of Kapuskasing and a Fox Moth from 1949 inland on the Albany River on the west coast of James Bay. But nothing of Hudson's Fairchild.

After the RCAF left, many civilians, including bush pilots, hunters, trappers, prospectors, and fishers, continued searching for the men, some by air and others on land. But their efforts, some noble, others seeking publicity and payment, turned up nothing. Despite the RCAF calling off its mission, the Minister of Lands and Forests said the search for the missing men would continue until they were found, dead or alive.

In Toronto, Smythe had stayed notably silent throughout the search and had been roundly criticized for it. But behind the scenes, he'd privately been pushing the provincial government to broaden the search. Now, he was pushing for it just to continue. Had it not been for Smythe, the search would've been much shorter in duration and much smaller in scope. Even when it was officially halted, Smythe didn't give up hope of finding his Stanley Cup hero. On October 2, eleven days before the Leafs were set to open the 1951–52 season, Smythe announced a $10,000 reward (about $120,000 seventy-five years later) for whomever found the missing men.

"We have been in constant touch with Dr. Lou Hudson and Bill's mother ever since they were reported missing," Smythe said. "Everything has been done up to now that could be done. We are making this announcement at a time when hundreds of hunters will be flocking to the North, and we hope the offer of a reward will result in a final all-out effort to locate either the men or their bodies before freeze-up time."

By then, with no indication as to the whereabouts of the missing men, rumors began to circulate about what had happened to them, including that Smythe had set the whole thing up as a publicity stunt for the Leafs. Other rumors had the men flying to Mexico or spotted in Florida.

One of the wildest rumors, however, was that the plane hadn't crashed at all but had, in fact, been flown across the country, using secret caches of fuel, and over the Pacific Ocean, to the Soviet Union, where Barilko, whose Ukrainian parents were born in Poland in what is now Belarus, had defected and was coaching players for Canada's communist Cold War rival. How Hudson fit into this conspiracy theory, beyond perhaps becoming the national team's dentist, was never made clear.

As winter loomed, the search eventually ended entirely. Barilko's mother continued to hold out hope that her son would one day walk through the front door, alive and well. She would go to church to pray, pleading for the return of her son.

"Please God, please tell me, one way or another, where my Billy?"

Barilko's mother sought the help of the Anglican bishop in Moosonee. On October 21, he broadcast a message in Cree from a radio station in Timmins asking the communities along James Bay, who knew the land better than any RCAF airman or civilian bush pilot, to search for her son. She also sought out fortune tellers, crystal gazers, and card, teacup, and palm readers, as well as other mediums. None of them amounted to anything. One such medium even wrote a letter to Smythe and the OPP in which she told them that Hudson and Barilko had crashed in the third lake from where they took off at Rupert House.

"I've consulted the cards many times and the answer is always the same," she said. "The trouble is, the plane was circling, and I don't know whether the lake is north, south, or east."

In Toronto, the Leafs opened their 1951–52 season with a 3–1 loss at Maple Leaf Gardens to the Black Hawks. In that evening's program, on the front cover and listed in the lineup was Barilko. In the dressing room, his sweater hung in his stall, awaiting his return.

In Barilko's absence, the Leafs had lost their heaviest hitter and a top penalty killer and shot-blocker. It showed. By early March 1952, the Leafs were well back of the first-place Detroit Red Wings. Smythe knew what the problem was. The Leafs were missing their strongman.

"We're weaker," Smythe said. "For one thing, we have no Bill Barilko to batter down the ramparts as he did in past years."

By the end of the regular season, the Leafs had limped to third place in the standings. In the playoffs, they were uneventfully swept in the semifinals by the eventual Stanley Cup champion Red Wings. They scored just three goals in those four games and were shut out twice.

A year to the day Barilko scored his overtime winner, Barilko Bros. filed for bankruptcy. The following September, nearly a year after her son had disappeared and been declared legally dead, Barilko's mother placed an in memoriam notice in the newspaper. In 1959, the family erected a headstone of Barilko next to his father's plot in Timmins Memorial Cemetery.

At Maple Leaf Gardens, Barilko's number 5 had long been taken out of circulation. It's never been worn since.

Discovery

The loss of Bill Barilko will be felt a great deal more than anyone realizes.

—Frank Boucher, New York Rangers general manager

ON JUNE 6, 1962, Frank Mahovlich was at Maple Leaf Gardens getting ready to take a ride through downtown Toronto with his teammates after winning the Stanley Cup just over a month earlier. As part of the festivities, the Toronto Maple Leafs had brought in retired captain Syl Apps to join the parade. Just as Mahovlich was about to jump into a convertible, he saw Apps coming toward him. Expecting congratulations, Mahovlich was stunned when the somber Apps told him the news.

"They just found Barilko's body."

Born in Timmins, Mahovlich had as a kid watched Barilko play in his hometown and had looked up to his hard-hitting forebear, whom he would follow from Timmins to Toronto to star with the Maple Leafs.

Upon hearing the news, the first thing Mahovlich realized was that Barilko's overtime goal in the 1951 Stanley Cup Final was the last time the Leafs had won the Cup until Mahovlich won his first of six in 1962.

In those intervening eleven years, Barilko's disappearance had remained a mystery. Every now and then, his name would pop up in a newspaper crossword puzzle or in the sports section in some article bemoaning the modern Leafs' lack of a true hard-hitting defenseman. Stories kept surfacing that the plane carrying Hudson and Barilko had crashed here or there in Northern Ontario. One had the men downed northeast of Kesagami Lake, another into Kabinakagami Lake west of Timmins, still another even as far south as around Sault Ste. Marie. But never did the North give up its long-kept secret. Until that day of the parade.

A week earlier, the morning of May 31, 1962, Gary Fields, a pilot with Dominion Helicopter Services, was on a routine flight about 72 kilometers (45 miles) north of Cochrane with timber technician Ray Paterick from the Ontario Department of Lands and Forests. The two were headed to New Post Creek to conduct a timber survey for a potential hydroelectric power project in the area. They were flying a thousand feet up, a few miles east of the Ontario Northland Railway, in Lot 24 of Concession III in McAlpine Township, near Island Falls on the Abitibi River, when something yellow caught Fields' eye near a dried creek bed in the dense forest below.

"There's a wrecked plane!" he shouted.

Fields dropped down to treetop level and saw what looked like a tail assembly and a pontoon embedded in the ground surrounded by a wall of trees. Both men believed it was an already charted plane wreck, so they thought nothing of it at the time. They were flying low, conditions were rainy with fog patches, and there were no landmarks nearby. Fields circled the wreckage twice but couldn't find anywhere close enough to land, so they didn't map it and made no note of it as they continued on with their day's work.

The next morning, Fields was back in Cochrane chatting with some colleagues during a coffee break when he offhandedly mentioned the wreckage he'd seen on his flight the previous day. Among them was Cochrane's district forester, Ted Hall. Fields knew little of the Barilko story, so he didn't quite understand when Hall and the others began peppering him excitedly with questions about the wreckage, which would've been off the line of flight Hudson and Barilko would've taken had they stayed on course from Rupert House to Timmins but well within the original search area back in 1951. What Fields and Paterick had thought was a known wreck was, in fact, undocumented.

Fields and Paterick attempted to relocate the wreckage using aerial photographs, while Hall ordered four aircraft into the air to search for the site. Bad weather delayed the search by one day.

The morning of June 2, Fields was back in the air with Paterick, along with forest protection supervisor Joe Shalla from the Department of Lands and Forests. Based on the aerial photos they'd had looked over the day before, Fields and Paterick decided to concentrate their search in Ireland Township. By then, the media had caught wind of the effort.

"Actually, we're not too sure we can find our way back to the same spot," Hall admitted to reporters. "There's always the possibility that what we saw were nothing more than some pieces of tin."

Hall called it "looking for a needle in a haystack," but he knew it was a needle that needed to be found.

Even though Fields had some idea of where he'd seen the wreckage, he hadn't charted it, and he knew he could easily fly over it again without seeing it, given the denseness of the surrounding forest. Day after day,

Fields and the other pilots retraced the route he'd flown on May 31, using a grid strip method for the search, while radio operator Mike Fera waited anxiously in the department's radio room back in Cochrane for word that the wreckage had been found. But every day, the pilots and their spotters returned tired, discouraged, and unsuccessful.

"An observer would have to be almost directly over the wreckage to see it," Fields told reporters. "If you are seventy-five to one hundred feet off to either side, you will miss it. All you need to do is blink and you're gone by it."

One of the other pilots was Sherwood "Woody" Pike from the Department of Lands and Forests in Hearst, Ontario. Like the others involved in the search, Pike pressed on, hoping to find the wreckage Fields had spotted. He would start at seven-thirty in the morning and go straight until four o'clock, stopping only for a ten-minute break on West Trappers Lake to give his spotters a rest. For eight hours, they would stare down into the same hypnotic green landscape, noses pressed against the windows of the five-seater Beaver, fighting nausea and drowsiness in the hot confines of the aircraft as they looked for a thirty-by-sixty burned-out clearing near a dried creek bed with a pontoon pointing toward the sky. There were thousands of such clearings. There were also numerous bleached logs that from a distance looked like aluminum floats when struck by the sun. On the second last day of the search, a reporter from Timmins joined Pike's team in the hunt to end the eleven-year mystery of Barilko and Hudson's disappearance.

"I tried to put myself in their shoes," Pike told him, "and fly the route around here that they would take if they were in trouble."

After a full day's work in the air, Pike and Fields would then sit down together and study aerial photographs, double-checking everything to make sure they hadn't missed anything.

On June 6, Fields took to the air again, this time with Hall, who rarely flew because he suffered badly from air sickness. They decided to go up at the same time of day as Fields' initial sighting on May 31 to re-create the lighting. This time, they focused on the eastern edge of McAlpine Township, due north of Ireland Township. The morning revealed nothing, so they began to fly back to base when around eleven o'clock Fields caught sight of some scraps of metal poking through a small opening in a stand of black spruce.

"What do I see here?" Fields yelled. "There it is!"

"Stop the plane!" Hall screamed. "Stop the plane!"

Hall then threw up his breakfast into his hat.

Fields tilted forward and wheeled around for a better look. There, in a dense clump of black spruce, they saw a pontoon, some mangled fuselage, and a patch of yellow. On his map, Hall circled a small lake and showed it to Fields, who added a dot on a creek near the wreckage. Wearing a wide smile, Fields decided to land near the lake so that they could relax for a moment before heading back to base.

"Even after all the talk, there was still a tendency to subconsciously associate the wreckage with old camps, stranded barges, et cetera," Hall noted. "Had there been a large patch of color, it would have shouted 'stop.' As it was, the impression was more like a dream you couldn't quite register. The only explanation is that I was not really expecting to see the object in that area, and it required a little bit of mental gear shifting to realize that the search was over."

It was the first and only time that Hall, who'd been directing search operations since Fields' initial sighting, had joined the hunt in the air.

"I guess you might say I was like a good luck charm for Gary," Hall told reporters. "Anyway, Gary redeemed himself. He spotted the wreckage last Thursday, and spotted it again today. Now no one can call him a liar."

For days, both men had been feeling the heat. Hall had been fielding calls at home at all hours of the day and night, and reporters had camped out on his lawn. After finding the wreckage, the horde of media finally left, and Hall hosted a small party at his home to celebrate the part that Gary "Eagle Eyes" Fields had played in solving the mystery. Later, Barilko's family would gift Hall a silver whisky flask that the Leafs had given Barilko for scoring his overtime goal.

"The pressure was really on to find it," Fields said. "I had seen it first, and when we couldn't find it again, people must have been wondering whether I'd been seeing things. And then when I spotted it, Ted and I just about jumped out of the machine."

After refueling, the first to go into the site, in early afternoon, was a search crew from Dominion Helicopter Services on contract to the Department of Lands and Forests consisting of Paterick, engineer Phil Weston, and helicopter pilot Ron Boyd, whom Fields had radioed to mark the location with toilet paper after finding the wreckage. Boyd found a place to land in a swampy area near a lake about 2.4 kilometers (1.5 miles) west of the crash site, where Weston hopped out to clear a landing area for the second helicopter. They then set out into the bush, using the sun to navigate because the density of the forest was throwing off their compass readings.

After nearly an hour of hacking their way through the bush, and trudging through knee-deep muskeg, they came upon the weather-beaten remnants of a small plane, nose down, its engine buried deep into the floor of the forest. The wings had been sheared off, and the tail section was bent over top. The branches that the plane had taken out in its death descent had covered the wreckage, making it difficult for anyone to spot from the air. One fuel tank had been ripped open and the other completely shattered. One pontoon, which stood on end like a tombstone, was the only part of the plane that hadn't sustained any significant damage. In what was left of the charred fuselage, they found the remains of two slightly scorched skeletons still strapped into their seats.

"The bones of the pilot were in the left seat covered in moss," Boyd said after returning from the crash site. "Barilko's bones were sprawled on top. The skull was shattered."

Under strict instructions from the Ontario Provincial Police, they were not to disturb the crash site. The three men began hiking back to their helicopter but lost their bearings in the dense bush and ended up a mile north. They managed to find their way back by listening for the second helicopter as it landed at the original landing site.

Led by Paterick and Shalla, Corporal Albert Duguid from the OPP detachment in Cochrane was next to get to the crash site, followed by two more plainclothes OPP officers. The bones were collected and placed in a haversack. A pocket watch and a belt buckle were taken out as well. From what was left of the fabric of the wings, they were able to piece together the registration number of what was a Fairchild 24: CF-FXT.

Eleven years after the plane had disappeared, the long-awaited radio call was finally sent out: "Identification positive."

"It is the plane, all right," Duguid told reporters back in Cochrane. "We were able to identify it from its official markings. The engine was buried in muskeg, but most of the fuselage was lying on the surface."

That evening, Barilko was once again the lead story on the CBC's national broadcast and front-page news in newspapers across the country:

THE LONG SEARCH ENDS—FIND BARILKO'S PLANE

SEARCH CREWS FIND SKELETON OF BARILKO IN PLANE WRECKAGE

11-YEAR PLANE MYSTERY SOLVED; FIND REMAINS OF TIMMINS MEN

At the time, Barilko's mother, by then sixty-three years old, was staying in London, Ontario, with her daughter, Anne, and son-in-law, Emil Klisanich. Anne had been told about the search since the wreckage was first spotted, but she chose not to tell her mother until definitive proof had been found. When the family finally received word that Barilko's remains had been recovered, after eleven long years, all Barilko's mother could say was, "My God, why couldn't this have happened long ago?"

"This has opened a lot of old wounds," Barilko's brother, Alex, told reporters after being notified of the news. "My sister and I are able to take it, but our mother is different. This has been a great shock to her."

The only consolation for their mother was closure.

"She didn't want to die not knowing the truth," Alex said.

Phyllis Hudson was living in Port Credit, Ontario, when she received the news.

"I gave up hope a long time ago," she said.

After spending about $1,000 every year following up on reports since his brother's disappearance, Lou Hudson was initially skeptical that the right plane had been found.

"Several times a year, screwballs swear to me that they've seen the plane," he said. "I had to check each one of them. I pray that this will finally end the mystery."

The only reporter to visit the crash site was Peter Worthington of *The Telegram* in Toronto. Fields shuttled him and his photographer, along with an official from the Department of Lands and Forests, close to the site. From there, they hiked through muskeg and swamp, accompanied by mosquitoes, blackflies, and deerflies, until they reached the plane.

When they got there, even though the skeletal remains had already been removed, they found shards of rib bones in a seeping bog and several teeth scattered about. Among the wreckage, the pontoons had been sliced open with an ax. Along with the rampant speculation that Barilko had defected to the Soviet Union was a wild rumor that Hudson, a dentist who used gold for crowns and fillings, had been smuggling gold out of the North and then flying it south into the United States. "High-grading," as it was called, wasn't an uncommon practice at the time and in the area. The overly large OPP presence during Operation Hudson back in 1951 was in part an offshoot of this rumor, though it was never made clear why Hudson would've flown so far north to Seal River. So when the plane was finally found, one of the first things the OPP did was take an ax to the pontoons in search of gold. They found nothing. Not even fish bones.

Two inspectors from the Canadian Department of Transport later flew and trekked to the location to determine the cause of the crash. The inspectors were supposed to return with a block and tackle to hoist the engine out of the bush, but they never did. In the end, the wings and tail were the only parts of the plane that were removed. Both were later destroyed, without informing the families of Barilko and Hudson. The rest of the wreckage was left to rust where it lay.

The human remains found at the scene were sent for identification. In those pre-DNA days, the pathologist in Cochrane was unable to positively identify them, only that they were two human skeletons, one of which was older than the other, and that they'd almost certainly died instantly from multiple skull fractures. A dentist could make no further determination. The OPP transported the remains to Toronto for examination at the Ontario attorney general's laboratory, but the lab there could conclude no better. Phyllis Hudson identified the watch as her husband's, and Alex Barilko did the same with the buckle of the belt he'd lent to his brother. Coupled with the airplane's call sign, the remains were positively identified as those of Henry Hudson and Bill Barilko.

On June 15, Barilko was buried in Timmins Memorial Cemetery, next to his father.

"We are told he had a smile for everyone except opposing forwards," said Reverend William Kitto in his eulogy.

Hudson was later buried in Toronto.

Although the eleven-year search had ended, the mystery remained, and still does to this day. The cause of the crash is believed to have been a combination of pilot inexperience and bad weather. Both may be true, but neither explains why or how the plane came down.

After the plane had been found, both Boyd and Fields gave their accounts of what they thought had brought it down in 1951.

"Tops of trees were sheared off," Boyd said, "and from the position of the wreck it looks as if the plane had stalled and spiraled straight down."

"It looked like the plane had cut a small swath when it went into the bush," Fields said. "It seemed as if Hudson had been flying low, ran out of gas, then tried to stretch his glide but failed."

Adding to the murkiness are the contradictory reports from Weston, who from his analysis of the wreckage believed "the plane caught fire but didn't explode," and Duguid, who said "it looked like one of the gas tanks had exploded."

There are also the vague conclusions of the official reports. The OPP files of the investigators in the case have long since been purged, which officers were required to do for any closed cases upon retiring until 1963, one year after the wreckage was found, so we'll never know what the police were able to determine about the crash or whether they were indeed looking for gold and if any was ever found. In its official report, the RCAF concluded that it was likely pilot inexperience that caused the crash. Over his five years as a licensed pilot, Hudson had accumulated only three hundred hours of total flying time and just five hours of dual instruction training, not nearly enough to fly into blistering headwinds, a darkening sky, and a rapidly descending ceiling while carrying a heavy load. An investigator from the unsuccessful search in 1951 came to the conclusion that the aircraft had probably plunged straight down in a near-vertical spin, boring into the floor of the thick northern forest, making the wreckage, hidden beneath the unbroken canopy, nearly impossible to spot from the air.

Given that the original search had turned up nothing, the RCAF had long believed that the plane probably crashed and sank into the water, likely in or around the area of Kesagami Lake, where the wreckage couldn't be seen from the sky. Many of the Cree in Northern Ontario and Northern Quebec believed the same thing, only that it'd crashed somewhere in James Bay shortly after its tenuous takeoff from Rupert House and sunk to the bottom of the bay.

Most of what is known about the crash comes from the official report of the Department of Transport. Although the plane had traveled about 274 kilometers (170 miles) southwest of Rupert House, it was found pointing north despite being on a flight path that was due south toward Timmins. The elevator trim had been set in the full nose-up position, which isn't normal for cruising. Given the damage to the propeller, the engine was indeed in operation when the plane crashed, which department representative A. J. Burleton testified to at an inquest into Hudson's death. The plane struck the ground on the pilot's side at a fifty-degree nose-down attitude and a twenty-five-degree left-bank angle, digging a hole three-feet deep and eight-feet wide. There were signs of a fire, possibly caused by an exploding fuel tank, which would suggest the plane hadn't run out of fuel after all. The details were so strange and inconclusive that the department could only conclude that the evidence was insufficient to make an official determination as to the cause of the crash. All that is known for sure is that no fault with the plane itself was ever found.

Competition among the authorities restricted cooperation that might've yielded clearer conclusions. Both the Department of Transport and the Department of Lands and Forests criticized the OPP for disturbing the wreckage. Because it was an aviation accident, the Department of Transport had jurisdiction.

On October 18, 1962, the inquest was held into Hudson's death. By then, many of the people associated with the original search in 1951 were scattered across the continent. The Crown made no attempt to summon them all together, calling only five witnesses: Corporal Duguid, doctors Albert Moore and A. F. Dungy, inspector Burleton from the Department of Transport, and Reverend Albert Williams, the Anglican missionary in Rupert House. It took the jury just thirteen minutes to conclude that Hudson had been an occupant in the plane crash and that he'd died from multiple head fractures. Barilko's case was excluded from the proceedings.

Shortly before she died in a Mississauga nursing home in February 1982, Barilko's mother talked to a reporter about the years her youngest son was missing. Every year, she expected him to show up at home and simply walk through the front door, right as rain. When he didn't, and another year passed, she would air out his clothes in expectation of seeing her son sometime the following year.

"All eleven years," she said, "I not miss one day I no cry for my Billy."

The Crash Site

Imagine sitting in the gray seats at the top of Maple Leaf Gardens and having to come down to ice level without using the stairwells, going over and around people, and every second seat having to zigzag. That's the density of the Hudson Plain. It's not like waiting in line for beer or the washroom. Here, you have to keep moving, because you have to make ground. That's how it is. It's slow and dense. I understood the context of where Barilko disappeared and wasn't found for such a long length of time, just because of the terrain. The landscape swallowed him up.

—"Back Roads Bill" Steer, founder of the Canadian Ecology Centre

WE WAIT BESIDE ISLAND Falls Generating Station, listening to the muted thunder of the turbines as the Abitibi River sweeps down through the spillways. Around us, the bush stretches outward in every direction. Mile after mile of black spruce and muskeg, the same indifferent country that once held one of the nation's most enduring secrets.

Finally, the helicopter appears in the distance, the sound rising and falling over the tree line like a pulse. It comes low across the dam toward us, through the spray and noise, using the road that led us here as its helipad. When it lands, pilots Chad Calaiezzi and Evan Green from Expedition Helicopters jump out to greet us. Chad's voice carries the roughness of gravel roads, while Evan's youthful timbre is soft and light as he walks us through every emergency procedure. Today, Evan is our pilot, Chad our guide. So, to make sure we're all listening to his much younger colleague, Chad reiterates Evan's instructions with the seriousness of someone who knows how quickly the bush punishes carelessness. When the briefing ends, we clamber into the helicopter.

The blades begin turning slowly, almost lazily, before gathering speed until the whole machine trembles with restrained force. Evan then lifts us into the great northern sky and banks east, pointing us toward the blinking label on the cockpit screen:

BARILKO

North of the great sweep of the Canadian Shield, the clearing in the bush where Bill Barilko met his fate has now become a place of pilgrimage. The steel skeleton of the Fairchild is gone, and with it the silent engine, the broken pontoons, the scraps of fabric. Relieved of its burden, the forest has begun to reclaim the place. Moss has thickened over the scars, the low-growing berry bushes have returned, and tamarack needles soften the ground where the aircraft struck. But a trickle of people keep coming. We are among them.

Stories like Barilko's travel further than statistics ever could. For Toronto Maple Leafs fans like longtime TV journalist Steve Paikin, Maple Leafs memorabilia collector Mark Fera, and me, the voyage starts long before the

152-kilometer (95-mile) drive north from Timmins along Highway 655, across the Trans-Canada Highway to Smooth Rock Falls, then up Highway 634, followed by the, at times, catapulting gravel road that leads to the five-minute flight from the hundred-year-old generating station. It begins with grainy photographs of the 1951 Stanley Cup Final, with Foster Hewitt's high-pitched call of Barilko's overtime goal in game five, and with clips of that magical moment in Maple Leafs history. It is further fed by the mythology that grew around the Leafs' long championship drought after Barilko's disappearance.

Leafs history bends around Barilko, like light around a black hole. The team wins the Stanley Cup in 1951 on his overtime goal against the Montreal Canadiens, then fails year after year afterward, as though the franchise itself had slipped under a curse. Leafs fans say this half-jokingly, but only half. Hockey fans are superstitious by nature, Leafs fans in particular. We need myths to explain our suffering. Barilko's story arrives already shaped. The hero rises, achieves glory, then vanishes into the wilderness.

Southern Ontarians romanticize the North because we encounter it only in fragments, on fishing trips, by campfires, in the sudden majesty glimpsed from highways. But places like this are indifferent to idealism. They don't care about fame. A man can score the most famous goal in Leafs history and still disappear here as quickly and completely as the flame of a match dropped into water. The North is filled with such stories. Planes crash, canoes overturn, hunters fail to return before freeze-up. The land is beautiful, but it doesn't negotiate. In that sense, the crash site isn't extraordinary at all. It is part of an older and harsher northern truth, that the wilderness doesn't care who anyone is when they enter it or whether those who are lost in it are ever found.

To reach the crash site requires pushing beyond roads and settlements, past the last conceit that human beings believed they could ever master the terrain. The location hid itself for years because the Hudson Plain possesses a terrifying patience. It can absorb metal, fire, and men without leaving so much as a scar visible from above. In 1951, searchers were forced to comb through thousands of square miles of it from the air, every monotonous mile of it a mirror of another.

In November 2022, I'd come here on assignment for *The Hockey News*, chasing a story that'd already been buried deep into the recesses of the Canadian imagination. Sixty years had elapsed since the plane was discovered, and thirty years had passed since a song we all know carried the name Barilko into living rooms, arenas, and on long highway drives across the country. That symmetry persuaded me to call Chad at Expedition Helicopters in Cochrane, Ontario, and ask him to shepherd me to the site of the story, into the heart of the legend.

I spent weeks on standby, waiting for the Northern Ontario triumvirate of weather, luck, and scheduling to align. Then with only a few days' warning, Chad called to say a narrow window had opened. If we were going, we had to leave before winter sealed the site shut.

The day dawned under a sky the color of tin. A foot of snow had fallen overnight, though the temperature hovered near freezing and the weather was windless, making the world feel strangely soft. The helicopter sat on the snow-darkened tarmac, black and gray beneath the dull light of the Northern Ontario sky.

From Cochrane to the landing site was a thirty-minute straight shot north of Chad's hometown. From there, it was a three-mile serrated trek to hike the last mile, as the crow flies, to the crash site. After a good two hours of struggling through thigh-high snow-covered brush, we stepped into a small clearing. Snow hung heavily from the surrounding trees. For the better part of an hour, we searched for a sign and a puck that'd been nailed to the trunk of a tree by earlier visitors, fragments of remembrance for the two men who'd died there. But winter had either buried or erased them. I didn't allow myself to register the disappointment. We were at the spot where Barilko had met his end, where the historical arc of the story stopped and the mythological began. That was enough for me.

Until four years later, in June 2026, when the bush, and the story, pulled me back in again.

From the air, the five of us stare out across the expanse all around us as the last trace of civilization dissolves into endless timber. Clouds conceal the sun, though the sky holds the hard, clear-blue clarity of an encroaching summer. Within minutes, the forest becomes overwhelming in its scale. The black spruce below are packed so tightly together that they resemble a vast woven green carpet. From above, the land seems sealed shut and secretive, incapable and unwilling of surrendering anything hidden beneath it. Only here, five hundred feet up, it is possible to understand how a wrecked floatplane could disappear for eleven years.

As we approach the coordinates, Evan settles the helicopter into a bog nearby where the trees grow stunted and sparse. The bush bends beneath the blades. The landing feels impossibly soft, as though the machine has lowered itself onto a feather bed. When the rotors finally stop, the silent bush closes around us.

Steve, Mark, and I jump out and begin sorting our gear for the trek into the forest. Chad stands over his GPS, checking his compass and keying in the coordinates of the crash site. The day feels borrowed. Only the night before, Chad had sent a message to our local fixer warning of an approaching storm front accompanied by a photograph of a shelf cloud advancing across the horizon. It looked less like weather than catastrophe, a dark, curling wall of vapor rolling toward town like a tsunami suspended in the sky. Had it lingered, months of planning would've unraveled within hours and scuttled our trek to the crash site. Instead, the storm spent itself in the darkness and moved on.

"Any animals out here?" Steve asks Chad.

"Yeah, we have a few," Chad replies. "I don't think we'll see too many today, but you never know. As far as hazardous animals, the only thing we really have to worry about is black bears, but even they're not generally predatory. We just want to make sure we don't stumble upon one and startle them."

"Have you seen one up here before?"

"I saw five of them on the way out here today," Chad says as he lets out a bellowing laugh.

"You're making me feel great. Let's go."

In the wake of the passing storm, the land seems to have exhaled. After weeks of late spring heat pressing down on the muskeg, the temperature has fallen into the mid-teens just days before summer is set to begin. A blanket of cloud hides the sun, and a light breeze drifts across the muskeg, stirring the black spruce. The blackflies, those tyrants of the northern woods, have largely retreated before the cooler air. The mosquitoes, however, remain undeterred. They rise from the muskeg in blurry squadrons and immediately discover any patch of exposed skin, settling upon us with the quiet confidence of creatures that know they belong here far more than we do. The three soft Southern Ontarians are all wearing bug nets: Steve and Mark are in near hazmat suits, while I'm wearing a balaclava, neck gaiter, head net, gloves, and sunglasses in a fruitless attempt to cover every inch of skin. The two hardy Northern Ontarians are dressed like they're heading to a local pub for lunch, not an afternoon hike into dense forest with swarms of mosquitoes.

"You northerners are a lot tougher than we are," I say to Chad and Evan.

"I got chewed really good the other day at my cottage trying to catch a big bass at the end of my dock with my daughter," Chad replies.

"Did you catch one?"

"No, he just kept stealing my hook. He was about that big. I was so focused that I looked down my arms and they were just bleeding. I was like, 'That's gonna itch for a week.'"

Around us stretches the stillness of the Hudson Plain. The crash site is less than a mile away, but distance in this part of the country means little. In the city, a mile is nothing. Along a road, it slips past almost unnoticed. Here, distance is measured in exhaustion, in soaked boots and burning thighs, in branches clawing at our sleeves, and black water rising over our ankles. It is as if even now the place resists being approached too easily.

Chad tells us that years earlier people had tried marking a route into the site, hopeful that it might ignite something permanent, a memorial, a destination, a preserved fragment of history. To him, the story deserves a place among the country's great legends. Forget about hockey. There is so much more of the national imagination held within it: the North, bush pilots, fishing camps, remote towns, impossible luck, regrettable determination. But there is no mass influx of tourists arriving with maps folded inside old biographies of Barilko. The nastiness and tenacity of the terrain has kept the crowds away.

Since the wreckage was found in 1962, there have only been four known visits to the crash site, and two other attempts to reach it. Those who've made it number no more than a few dozen, and all have come by helicopter. The handful who haven't but tried have come by motorcycle along unmapped logging roads or by snowmobile over trails that disappear into drifting snow, only to be thwarted by the muskeg when forced to continue on foot.

"Mark, would you rather be doing this or sitting by the pool sipping a margarita?" Steve asks as we squeeze through a narrow section of tangled bush.

"Who, me? I'd rather be doing this, buddy," Mark replies. "I'm not gonna lie."

Mark wouldn't miss this for the end of the world. His devotion to the story is unconditional. For Steve and I, our fealty to it is merely on the plane of idealism, as a story, a legend. Mark's is materialism, a loyalty to all of the objects attached to it. At his home on the outskirts of Toronto, among the largest collection of game-used and vintage rare Maple Leafs memorabilia in the world, Mark has some three hundred artifacts related to Barilko that he either painstakingly tracked down himself or fatefully received from others. Less collected than summoned, they've gathered around Mark as if the story has chosen its next guardian, from signed programs of the Hollywood Wolves and a copy of one of Barilko's contracts with the Leafs to the last puck Barilko potted into an NHL net and the Stanley Cup ring he never received.

After the plane was finally discovered in 1962, the wreckage remained at the crash site, rusting away season after season, in the clump of forest where it lay. In all that time, the families of the two men who'd died there had assumed the authorities had removed it all those years ago. It wasn't until Dr. John Shaw, who'd taken over Dr. Henry Hudson's old dental practice in Timmins, set out to rediscover the location forty-three years later that they learned most of the wreck was still there. By then, the site had to be found all over again because the original coordinates had been logged incorrectly when the plane was discovered, marking a patch of swamp instead nearly a mile away.

Shaw teamed up with a lumber company that owned the license to harvest the area. After several flights to pinpoint the location, with help from local historians Mel Robbins and Allan Shier, they managed to find the wreckage from the air on March 31, 2005. Armed with the correct coordinates, Shaw put together a ground party to trek to the site on the fifty-fourth anniversary of Barilko's overtime goal that April, but bad weather forced him to wait a month. Finally, on May 20, 2005, after years of research and nine months of planning, Shaw hiked in, along with helicopter pilot Dave Marko, journalist Ken Pagan, and two employees from the lumber company. Leading the way with his GPS was forestry technician Roland Szyska, and marking their trail, wearing a Leafs shirt, was operations manager Tim Schmidt, who was born in 1967, the last year the Leafs had won the Stanley Cup. As they neared the crash site, Szyska turned to the seventy-year-old Shaw, who was bringing up the rear of the group.

"John, do you want to come up here?"

The group stayed silent as Shaw moved up to the front, working his way through some branches, and pulled out his video camera. There, about ten feet away, was one of the pontoons standing upright in the muskeg. Shaw continued to the site, and the rest of the group followed. When they reached wreck, everyone set their packs down and stared at the rusted remains. No one said a word until Shaw broke the silence.

"Tough luck, Henry," was all he said.

The group looked over the wreckage, uncovering the engine, a wing strut, part of the propeller, some of the plane's yellow fabric, and the handle of a paddle Barilko and/or Hudson would've used on their fishing trip. On a nearby tree, they then put up a sign bearing an image of a yellow Fairchild 24 model G underneath an inscription that honored the two men who died there:

At this location
August 26, 1951
Bill Barilko
and
Dentist
Henry Hudson
Lost their Lives
Rest in Peace

The ground continues to shift beneath our feet as Steve, Mark, and I plod on between Chad and Evan. The trees crowd together around us in dense black ranks, thin spruce trunks packed so tightly their lower branches weave into walls. Beneath them, the muskeg trembles under our weight. Some patches hold firm while others suddenly give way, submerging us to the knees in black water.

We tread slowly because there is no other way to move. Every step must be tested before we trust it. We place our boots carefully on hummocks of moss only to feel them sag and buckle beneath us like wet mattresses. It leaves us breathing hard, our hearts hammering from what should be nothing more than walking.

The farther we push into the forest, the more exhausting the terrain becomes. Branches brush across our shoulders, shooting needles down our collars. Water seeps into boots advertised as waterproof. Chad moves ahead steadily, warning us away from hidden roots and pockets of water. At times, the bush seems so thick as to be nearly impassable. Alders tangle together, and cedar branches knit themselves into walls. Having been to the crash site three times already, Chad speaks of the sheer expense of flying people here and of how often strangers call asking him to take them in. If only they knew how much it truly costs to reach it.

"How does this trek compare to the one you did fifteen years ago?" Steve asks Chad.

"Well, it's the same walk through the bush."

"Easier? Harder?"

"About the same. It hasn't changed one bit."

"Do you remember what you were thinking when you got to this point through your journey?"

"There was some excitement or anticipation of what was at the end. But frankly, until you actually come across it or get to the location, and I would imagine it was very similar when they were searching for it from the air, you don't really know what you're expecting until you get there. There's no real excitement until you actually find it."

Chad first came here in December 2005, seven months after Shaw's trip, when he guided a group of family and friends to the wreckage. His second trip came six years later.

On October 16, 2011, Chad and fifteen others set down near the crash site to bring what remained of the wreckage home to Timmins. The mission was led by Shaw and underwritten by local businessman and former pro goalie Bill Hughes, but it carried the weight of something larger than logistics or financing. It drew in those bound to the story by blood, by place, and by history. Among them were Mike Mulryan, Kevin Vincent, and Wayne Bozzer from Barilko's hometown, Barilko's cousin Sandra Cattarello, and Archie Chenier, then eighty-six, who was supposed to be on that final fishing trip instead of Barilko.

By then, sixty years had passed since the plane had crashed. The forest had kept its secret, but mining roads were pressing inward, and logging operations were edging closer. There was a growing worry that if the wreckage wasn't recovered soon, parts of it would be lost either to the harmless curiosity of fans or the greed of souvenir hunters. With the blessing of both families, the group resolved to lift out what remained and bring it home.

"Not a piece stays in the bush," Hughes told Mulryan in the lead-up to the trip. "Not a piece. Everything comes out. Everything."

The weather that morning was Northern Ontario's usual autumn admixture of cold rain and bursts of snow. Some in the group flew the 75 kilometers (47 miles) from the headquarters of Expedition Helicopters in Cochrane. The rest, like Steve, Mark, and I today, shuttled in on the short flight from Island Falls. The helicopter set them down about a mile from the site. From there, they moved on foot, with six of the sixteen of them carrying hatchets or axes to hack their way through the bush. The others followed behind, including Chenier, who carried an old wooden Louisville hockey stick as a tribute to Barilko. He would later gift each member of the group a walking stick with the words "Hudson–Barilko Recovery Project" engraved on it and the date of the expedition. In the spirit of Chenier's tribute, I've brought along my own bladeless wooden stick for the hike, wrapped from top to bottom in black stick tape.

"Looking for a walking stick?" I ask Mark as he picks up a branch off the ground.

"It's just sitting here," he replies, "looking like it needs a purpose."

As the sixteen-strong expedition team hiked in, rain drifted into flurries and back again. It took them two hours to hike in. What remained of the plane lay within a 10-meter (33-foot) radius, completely surrounded on all sides by trees 40 meters (131 feet) high. The foliage had enclosed it like a coffin. The plane had been scattered and half-claimed by the earth, metal and memory tangled in roots and soil. One pontoon, still intact, stood upright, leaning against a tree, its nose buried. The other was in pieces. Both bore conspicuous ax marks. The seven-cylinder Warner

Scarab engine was embedded into the ground. A small stubborn tree had grown improbably through it, life threading itself through ruin.

For a moment, no one spoke. It was time to reflect, to remember that two men had lost their lives there. Shaw consecrated the area, then Cattarello, who was only eleven years old when her cousin died, gathered the group and led them in prayer, her voice quavering in the cold air until tears took over and the words trailed away.

"Just one small blessing here," she began. "Glory be to the Father, the Son, and the Holy Spirit. As there was at the beginning, is now, and ever shall be, world without end. Amen. Bless this ground in memory of Dr. Henry Hudson and my cousin, hockey star Billy Barilko."

Cattarello then held up a vial about the length of a middle finger, a sardonic salute to those who succumbed to the rampant rumors of high-grading that followed the two men to their graves and beyond.

"We have a little bit of gold to put somewhere in here," she said.

Shaw followed, reading A. E. Housman's poem "To an Athlete Dying Young." His voice carried the words softly through the trees:

The time you won your town the race
We chaired you through the market-place;
Man and boy stood cheering by,
And home we brought you shoulder-high.

To-day, the road all runners come,
Shoulder-high we bring you home,
And set you at your threshold down,
Townsman of a stiller town.

When it was Hughes' turn to speak, the group gathered around him like a hockey team huddling in front of its captain at a critical moment in the game that called for both inspiration and instruction. The mission was always meant to be more than just a recovery effort.

"This is all part of what we hope to accomplish today as far as planting the seed in a couple of different ways, where kids coming out of Northern Ontario feel good about coming out of Northern Ontario," Hughes said. "I think the North does something to us, and I know that it's good. And Bill Barilko exemplified that with the Northern Spirit that he carried with him famously."

Then began the work, quietly, almost instinctively. They had no power tools to help them, only axes, shovels, and their hands. They dug and pulled, freeing pieces of the aircraft that had lain buried for sixty years. The labor was slow, physical, unglamorous.

At one point, Mulryan stopped to have a cigarette.

"Did you ever think you'd be sitting here?" someone asked him.

"No, never," Mulryan said as he leaned against a downed tree in the clearing. "When I first got in here, the hair on the back of my neck was standing straight up."

By afternoon, what remained of the plane had been gathered and secured in a heavy net for lifting, even the three-hundred-pound engine. Freeing the upright pontoon, filled with water, from the muskeg's iron grip revealed the left rubber boot of a hip wader from that fateful fishing trip.

Chad, who'd hiked back to the helicopter, then ferried the wreckage out in three separate trips. Before the group left, Mulryan nailed a Leafs puck to a tree beneath the sign Shaw had erected six years earlier. It was an offering as much as a marker.

With the wreckage back in Timmins, at the edge of the lake that saw Barilko and Hudson depart but never return, the group paused once more before concluding the mission. Using two cups from a local Tim Hortons, Shaw and Mulryan poured water drawn from Porcupine Lake over the aircraft's floats. The ritual was improvised but quite unknowingly carried a quiet symmetry of something long overdue. It wasn't until half an hour later, as they were putting the wreckage into storage, that the group was jarred by the coincidence of their simple act of closure.

"Oh my god, do you know what we just did?" one of them said. "Tim Horton replaced Bill Barilko on the Leafs' blueline."

With the wreckage safely stored at a secret location outside Timmins, the task shifted from recovery to remembrance. The group that'd brought it home searched for a place where the story could live on, somewhere the fragments could be seen, understood, and held in context. They approached the Hockey Hall of Fame, the Timmins Victor M. Power Airport, the Timmins Museum National Exhibition Centre, the Timmins Sports Heritage Hall of Fame, and the Canadian Bushplane Heritage Centre. Each, for its own reasons, declined. Some because of space or money, others afraid of appearing morbid and raising ghosts from the past.

For a brief moment, there was hope. A meeting with Maple Leaf Sports & Entertainment opened the possibility of a traveling exhibit, something that could carry the story across the country, from city to city, and rink to rink, to future generations. But the momentum was fragile, the moment fleeting. Within days, and quite independently, MLSE's president resigned. Emails went unanswered, and the thread unraveled.

So, the wreckage remained in storage, recovered at last from the bush but still waiting, in its own way, for a final resting place.

The lack of interest in the wreckage remains one of the most confounding elements of the story. It is, in every tangible sense, the central artifact of one of the country's most enduring narratives. Yet no one stepped forward to claim it. Not in Toronto, where Barilko became a legend. Not in Timmins, where he was born and now rests. Not anywhere across the country that had once announced his name in headlines and carried him in its memory.

In this way, the fate of the wreckage mirrors the fate of the story itself. For all its weight, for all its mythic qualities, there is remarkably little that marks Barilko's place in the national consciousness. This is the man who scored the most famous goal in Leafs history in one of the greatest moments the game has ever produced. Yet his presence today is found only in fragments. There is no statue cast in his likeness, no monument to fix his story in place. His name doesn't mark a school, a street, a park, or an arena, not even in his hometown. There is no permanent exhibit to house the remnants of his life, no major film, biopic, or TV series to carry his story forward. What remains instead are traces: a pair of biographies that are both now out of print, a couple of songs that are more than thirty years old, two short-lived video features that are no longer available for view, and a screenplay that never saw the light of day. It is as though the story persists not in what has been built around it, but in what has been left undone, a legacy defined as much by absence as by memory.

For more than eight years, the wreckage remained in storage. The parts were protected from the elements but not variations in temperature and humidity. The wreckage was corroding, and the story was dying with it. With no one to ferry the plane to its next stop, Fera offered to give it a permanent home. Vincent and others from the retrieval expedition talked. They knew they'd taken the story as far as they could. It was someone else's turn to shepherd it now.

Vincent met with Fera.

"We've decided you're the guy to carry this forward," he told him. "We'll give it to you to decide what's best."

In winter of 2020, Fera drove up to Timmins for his first look at the plane's remains. He was joined by a representative of MLSE and the mayor of Timmins. The weather called for big snow. They weren't even sure they could get to the shed where the wreckage was waiting. Then Fera's phone rang. It was Vincent.

"You won't believe it," Vincent said. "There's snow on either side of the city but not at the site."

Fera smiled.

"Bashin' Bill is giving us a path to the net," he replied.

When they arrived, Fera found a brand new $100 bill. There was no one around, and the nearest house was about 300 meters (984 feet) away. Fera held up the bill.

"Boys, Bill is buying us lunch."

When Fera pulled out of town with the wreckage rattling in the bed of his pickup, a rainbow arced low across the frozen road, vivid against the iron winter light. He drove toward it in silence, feeling, with the strange certainty men sometimes take for grace, that Barilko was giving him his blessing. Today, among a sea of blue-and-white Maple Leafs memorabilia, the battered remains of the plane hold pride of place in Fera's suburban shrine to the team and the story, resting on a wooden platform clothed in gold and carefully arranged atop a bed of mock moss and earth, as though Northern Ontario itself followed the plane to Toronto, unwilling to release its claim.

As the five of us plunge deeper into the forest, direction becomes meaningless, and distance deceives us constantly. A stand of trees that appears a hundred feet away takes twenty minutes to reach. The landscape repeats itself endlessly. It is the same crooked spruce, the same pale lichen, the same stagnant pools reflecting the northern sky. We understand immediately how easy it would be to get lost in here. Everything about the Hudson Plain conspires against orientation.

The silence unsettles us more than the mosquitoes. We think of Barilko as we walk, though not as people remember him now. Out here, the North strips away all romance. The mythology of the famous goal, the photographs, the legend surrounding his disappearance all fall away in the face of this interminable landscape. We find ourselves thinking instead about the final moments aboard that plane, the endless forest below the wings, the realization for the two men that there was nowhere to land, no way to walk out, no chance to be found.

"I've tried not to think about this too much," Steve says. "But the reality is that when Henry and Billy were flying, and whatever happened happened, and they were about to crash, you can just imagine what was going through their heads."

"For sure," Chad replies. "That being said, I'm not sure they actually got the moment to think about it. I imagine they were trying to stretch the glide if the engine quit. We don't even know that for sure, but I think he was trying to get to the lake nearby. I'm not a fixed-wing pilot, but I believe when you stall an aircraft it comes down pretty quick."

As uncomfortable as we are, I realize that to reach this mythic site by helicopter is merely to visit a tragedy. There are those who refuse this course of action, who instead remain on the ground to measure themselves against the same immensity that hid Barilko for so long. Every seven years, it seems, some stubborn outdoorsman, or some knot of them, shoulders a pack and supplies, even oddities like a book of poetry and a surfboard, and then ventures into the Hudson Plain believing, against all evidence to the contrary, that endurance, woodsmanship, and sheer will can close the last impossible miles without aid of the air. Perhaps what draws them isn't really the crash site at all, or even Barilko himself, but the increasingly rare chance to enter a landscape so vast and indifferent that a person can still vanish inside it and feel, for a little while, the old

Canadian terror and romance of being lost in pursuit of a legend. That, and to accomplish something no one has ever done: reach the crash site overland.

In February 2014, Oliver "Brokentooth" Solaro walked into the office of Expedition Helicopters in Cochrane searching for someone who knew something of the crash site. He wasn't there to hire a helicopter. He wanted to know how to get there by land.

A pilgrim in pursuit of Barilko, Solaro had begun his trek north at a Ryerson Rams home game at Mattamy Athletic Centre in Toronto. He wasn't there to cheer on the Rams but to see them off the ice and the rest of the crowd out of the arena. Once everyone was gone, he ambled down to ice level, dressed incongruously in motorcycle gear, and proceeded to walk out to center ice. There, he reached into his pocket and pulled out a loonie. Under the suspicious gaze of security guards, he laid it carefully on the center ice dot to absorb the setting where Barilko scored his Stanley Cup–winning goal in 1951.

With the loonie stored safely in his pocket, Solaro jumped onto his Kawasaki KLR, "Agatha," and navigated Toronto's Friday rush hour as commuters cast curious stares at the sight of a motorcycle on the highway in the middle of winter. He stopped for the night at home in Williamsford, Ontario, near Owen Sound, where he maintains a blue-collar existence as a former motorcycle dealer turned jack-of-all-trades, and then carried on the next morning to Cochrane, where he met with Calaiezzi. Knowing how quickly the winter woods north of town can reduce even the best-laid plans to waste, Calaiezzi was skeptical but willing to help Solaro, if only to ensure the man would return from the bush alive.

By then, years before he would be diagnosed with ADHD in his mid-fifties, Solaro had undertaken several of the two-wheeled adventures that have since seen him branded "Canada's Ice Road Biker" for his winter forays into nowhere Northern Ontario and beyond. One of his first was driving his motorcycle along the world's longest ice road, the 752-kilometer (467-mile) Wapusk Trail, which runs between the towns of Gillam in northeastern Manitoba and Peawanuck in northwestern Ontario. Another came during the apex of COVID-19 restrictions, when he hauled a thousand pounds of donated dog food behind a converted motorcycle, equipped with a front ski, across northwestern Ontario and up to Churchill, Manitoba, in order to feed local mutts after the rail line that carries goods to the town had been washed out. His most ambitious adventure would come in the waning days of the pandemic, when a documentary team filmed a pilot of Solaro beginning an attempt to reach the North Pole by motorcycle.

On the surface, his attempt to reach the crash site by motorcycle and then snowshoe, a quest Solaro would later describe as Salvador Dalí and Hunter S. Thompson collaborating on the next *Jackass* movie, seemed smaller in scope and so easier in effort than any of his other northern adventures. The Hudson Plain would soon prove otherwise.

For Solaro, the journey had narrowed itself into a single, almost holy necessity, an impulse whispering, "You have to do this." He wasn't seeking glory or searching for witnesses. The world didn't need to know he'd gone there. It was enough that he would know. Enough that, years later, he could say to himself: "I stood there, where Henry and Bill met their makers. They saw the end of the world right there."

The next morning, Solaro drove 90 kilometers (56 miles) north under a washed-out sky, following an unmapped logging road that unspooled endlessly through the timber until he got as close as 7 kilometers (4 miles) east of the crash site. A crew of French-Canadian loggers promised to keep an eye on Agatha while he was gone. He left her half-consumed by a snowdrift, white being heaped on the bike like the slow work of a burial. Then he strapped on his snowshoes and trudged into the bush.

His equipment was pitiful given the wilderness he faced. A $50 sleeping bag was all he had to keep himself warm in the minus-thirty-something nights amid the muskeg, while a battered book of Robert Service poems was tucked away like a private prayer. The poetry, more than either his GPS unit or his video equipment, felt necessary.

What Solaro wanted was contact. He wanted to hear the site itself speak to him, to move through the country where the story had ended and let the shape of it settle into him. The legend had taken hold of him and remained there, luminous and unfinished, exerting its pull on him through weather and distance, effort and exhaustion.

The crash site looked deceptively close on paper. But nothing in the Hudson Plain permits a straight line. The terrain forced him into a slow, endless zigzag.

Solaro threaded himself between trunks and brush, testing each step before trusting it, careful not to disappear into the dark pools concealed beneath the snow. At times, the muskeg clutched greedily at his boots, as though the earth itself wished to keep him there. Every ten steps or so plunged him waist-high into champagne powder snow that hid a tangled terrain of brush that poked at his chassis and a root system that held him tight. Exhausted from the day's hike and soaked with sweat, he'd barely made it a mile before having to set up camp. With no tent, he made a makeshift bed of black spruce and slept beneath the black, starry skies of Northern Ontario.

Morning brought more of the same, and afternoon fared no better. Not yet even halfway to the crash site, Solaro spent another night in the minus-whatever weather with Service as his bedfellow. Upon waking, he briefly flirted with the idea of plodding ahead but decided to turn back, vowing to one day return.

Crestfallen, Solaro choked back tears for being so close. But it wasn't meant to be, not on that day, not in this land.

Time for plan B.

With the loonie still in his pocket, Solaro decided that if he couldn't lay it at the crash site, he would do so at Barilko's grave. So he hiked back to Agatha, thanked the loggers for watching over her, and set off for Barilko's hometown.

When he arrived at Timmins Memorial Cemetery, he found it far larger than expected. With many of the headstones buried in several feet of snow, he spent much of the rest of the day walking along the laneways of the sprawling cemetery and back and forth in between the graves, scanning them for any sign of the plot holding Barilko's bones. Eventually, a letter "O" above the snow caught his eye. A quick brush of the snow revealed it to be the resting place of Barilko's parents, Steve and Faye. His heart pounded in his chest. Solaro scoured away the snow from an adjacent headstone. A small circular photo revealed a black-and-white image of Barilko, adorned in a white Leafs sweater.

After stripping out of his motorcycle gear, Solaro pulled out his journal and a bottle of single malt Scotch. Wearing nothing but a kilt, black sweater, winter boots, and an Indiana Jones hat, he sat down in the snow to sip and scribble while leaning against Barilko's headstone. Before leaving, he pulled the loonie out of his pocket and laid it on the base. He then placed a hand upon the freezing granite and softly said four words to the legend.

"Thank you, Bill. Goodbye."

After a while as we hike, time ceases to matter. We stop checking our watches. Progress here can't be measured in hours and minutes. Instead, it is about obstacles overcome. We cross a creek on a rotting trunk slick with moss, force open a dense wall of alder, and savor a brief stretch of firmer ground where our boots don't disappear into water. We emerge from that section, soaked and scratched and exhausted, only to see another identical stretch waiting ahead.

More than seven years after Solaro left this land defeated, another hardy Northern Ontario outdoorsman with a nickname befitting a Barilko excursion sought out the legend overland to the site of the story's end. On December 9, 2021, "Back Roads Bill" Steer left Timmins with his friend Brian Emblin, passing the recently erected Barilko billboard on their way out of the city east along Highway 101. At five o'clock in the pitch-black morning, the headlights only slightly illuminated Barilko's vibrant smile next to his clenched, celebratory right fist. In the car, among the pile of snowmobile and hiking gear, the two men carried with them a sign to be placed at the crash site:

Bill Barilko . . . not a fallen and forgotten Leaf.

On his outdoor adventures, Steer had gone much farther afield, both overseas, trekking across a glacier in Greenland and to Annapurna Base Camp in Nepal, as well as throughout Northern Ontario, including a trip to the northernmost boundary between Manitoba and Ontario. On that provincial expedition, Steer ended up seeing twenty-one polar bears, including the one his Cree guide had to scare away from their rickety cabin with his rifle after it awoke them from their slumber.

From Timmins, Steer and Emblin drove north to Smooth Rock Falls and then up to Abitibi Canyon, where they linked up with two employees from Ontario Power Generation. The four of them then put on their snowmobile suits in one of the garages and set out into the minus 30°C (minus 22°F) morning.

Behind one snow machine, they pulled a sleigh full of emergency equipment, including extra clothes, a chainsaw, an ax, a folding saw, rope, and a satellite communication device. They also brought their own $50 purchase, a surfboard bought at a garage sale. Not to surf the snowdrifts but to ford a creek near the crash site. Falling through the ice that day would've carried potentially fatal consequences. All this to put up their own sign in honor of Barilko.

"That goddamn surfboard has come off the back of the snowmobile again," one of the OPG employees said.

Over the previous two years, Emblin had done reconnaissance in search of the closest, most direct route to the crash site by snowmobile. He found it at a trail 35 kilometers (22 miles) south of Abitibi Canyon. When the four of them reached it that morning, it hadn't been used, so the snow was neither packed nor groomed.

"How the heck are we going to get through this?" Emblin said as the group stared at the trackless route ahead.

The four of them had to churn their way through the snow, stopping repeatedly to chop down a tree or maneuver their snowmobiles around windfalls. Eventually, close to the crash site but unable to go any farther by machine, they parked their snowmobiles, switched out their snowsuits for lighter hiking attire, slipped on their snowshoes, and strapped on small daypacks. With the surfboard in tow, they set off into the frozen muskeg.

Initially, they made good gains over relatively open ground, but the terrain quickly turned against them. The combination of deep snow and dense spruce sent them off course. Getting through it themselves was hard enough, but hauling the surfboard was quickly depleting their energy reserves.

"This is the second fucking stupidest idea I've ever had," Steer said.

"Second?" the other three said in unison.

"Well, I'm sure there'll be another one."

With daylight fading, the four of them had made it only as far as McAlpine Lake. Still 4.2 kilometers (2.6 miles) from the crash site, Steer heeded the "safety first" advice he regularly gives his students as founder of the Canadian Ecology Centre in North Bay, Ontario.

"This is far as we're going to get today, guys," Steer told the rest of the group.

No one else said a word. They were disappointed, but they knew he was right. As they turned back, they left the surfboard behind for another attempt still to come.

"How're we doing so far?" Steve stops to ask Chad. "Where are we?"

"Not bad," Chad replies amid birds chirping around us. "We've traveled almost a kilometer. As you can see, we're getting close to the creek, which was beside the wreckage, and there's a lot of alders and thick undergrowth. We've got a few downed trees here that are problematic, so everybody walk slowly and carefully. Ginger steps. Make sure there's something to support you before you put your weight on it. Every time I've come in here, I've never followed the same path, ever. It ain't pretty in here, gentlemen. But the birds are lovely."

On the final few meters of our trek, the forest begins to change. The trees thin out and the muskeg opens up. We feel a shift in the atmosphere, and the silence deepens into something almost ceremonial as we close in on the coordinates.

Before proceeding, we stand for moment, breathing heavily from the hike and listening to the wind move through the black spruce. Then we move forward. We arrive in silence.

For anyone who's stood where the plane came down, the story becomes smaller, though no less meaningful for that. At the site of his demise, the larger-than-life story of Bill Barilko becomes human-sized. Only here can it truly be understood.

"Do you feel like we're on the spot?" Steve asks Chad.

"Oh yeah, we're definitely in the immediate vicinity," Chad replies. "Obviously, we lifted everything out of here in 2011 with the helicopter.

The GPS is only so accurate in this dense bush, so we could be off by a dozen meters or something like that."

"We're looking for a tree with a sign on it, right?" Steve asks Chad of the sign Shaw and his crew put up in 2005. He then rummages through his backpack. "I gotta show you something. You're gonna recognize it, and you tell me what it is."

"Oh, I've seen this," Chad says. "This was in here. This was the Department of Transport's sign."

In June 1962, having gathered everything they believed the crash site could yield, every piece of evidence, every observation destined for the report that would follow, the investigators turned their backs on the shattered landscape and performed one final act of officialdom. They offered neither mourning nor remembrance, only administration, marking the location with the cold calculus only government bureaucracy can calibrate.

Steve reads from the original sign:

WRECKAGE OF FAIRCHILD 24. CF-FXT
CRASHED 26 AUG. 1951. FOUND AND
INVESTIGATED JUNE 1962 BY ACCIDENT
INVESTIGATION DEPARTMENT
DEPARTMENT OF TRANSPORT OTTAWA.

"It's ironic that they made this plaque to indicate the investigations that took place to find the wreckage of the plane, but they don't mention Barilko, they don't mention Hudson," Steve says. "That's kind of strange, don't you think?"

"Yeah, you're right," Chad replies. "No mention of Hudson or Barilko."

"That's why we're here," Steve continues. "To remember them. We appreciate the investigators, but we're here to remember the two guys that died that day. I can't help but hear the birds chirping in the background, and the sun is shining and it's a lovely day and we've been trekking for the last hour and a half or so, and just the contrast between the beauty of this scene and what happened on that day back in 1951. It's eerie, I find."

"Agreed. It would've been a whole lot of noise in a hurry and then silence again."

Shaw's sign replaced the original to atone for its sin of omission. The only physical indicator that two men died here, along with the puck Mulryan nailed to the same tree, it is all that marks the crash site, and all that is needed to do so. The North doesn't preserve tragedy the way cities do. There are no fences here, no polished monuments, no plaques fixed to stone. The wilderness absorbs tragedy, folding human catastrophe into the larger silence of the land. Standing at the site, after everything it's taken merely to walk the final mile, we begin to understand this.

Two truths compete for the crash site. One is legend, the other is silence. The site strips celebrity away from tragedy. Here, Barilko isn't frozen forever in newspaper photos or immortalized victorious in the overwrought mythology of hockey. The bush has a way of reducing every narrative to its essentials. Two men flew far north for a fishing trip. Something went wrong, and they died alone beneath a canvas of green, hidden from searching eyes in the sky and pleading prayers on the ground.

In the bush, Barilko becomes mortal again. A twenty-four-year-old man who died far from home. So too for Hudson, a northern flyer who knew the land intimately and still couldn't survive it that day.

The five of us split up and wander through the trees in search of Shaw's sign and Mulryan's puck. As I walk around the area, sore, sick, and sapped of energy, the silence of the northern bush presses inward. I try to understand what's drawn me back here. It isn't spectacle. There is no wreckage left to see, no tourist attraction hidden in the bush. It is the story itself. Others before me have come for different reasons, but they were all drawn by the same impulse. The forest took Barilko, but it never fully let him disappear. Here among the trees, I understand why I've returned. It isn't to come to the location again, but to stand, even for just a moment, inside the story, at the site of its end, one last time.

"No sign of the sign," Chad says as he continues searching. "Frustrating, eh, Ronnie?"

"Yeah, I'm oh for two now," I reply.

Standing at the site of the crash, back in November 2022, I found myself unexpectedly thinking more about Hudson than Barilko. At the time, I was Hudson's age when he died. His memory now survives mostly in the margins of another man's legend. Hudson belonged to a generation of northern professionals who helped build communities from the ground up. As a respected dentist, he earned a reputation for competence, steadiness, and public spirit, tending to the needs of a mining town that was itself still young and growing. Beyond his practice, he was known as an avid outdoorsman, drawn to the wilderness that surrounded the region and embracing the self-reliance and adventure that northern life demanded. Friends knew him as a capable fisherman, a man equally at ease in a dental office as on the waterways of the Hudson Plain. Yet history is rarely democratic. Barilko carried into the wilderness a story already burnished by glory. Hudson carried only the quieter dignity of an accomplished life. Unfortunately for his memory, history, like a novelist in search of a protagonist, chose the figure whose fate completed a dramatic arc. As Barilko's name echoed across generations, Hudson's receded into the shadows.

Hudson was on the cusp of fifty when he died. Chad, Steve, Mark, and I are all on the far side of it now, while Evan is only three years shy of the age when this godforsaken ground snuffed out Barilko at twenty-four years old.

"Do you know the Barilko story well, Evan?" I ask him.

"Yeah, I first learned about it from The Hip," he replies.

I smile at the thought that "Fifty Mission Cap" continues to carry the story onward, passing it from one generation to the next like a flame sheltered against the wind, preserving it in melody long after memory alone would've let it fade. Decades after it was released, the song still bears the weight of the legend, transporting it across time in a way that newspaper clippings, memorial plaques, and official histories never could.

"Are you a Hip fan?"

"I'm quite a large Hip fan."

"I'm glad to hear that. Next generation Hip fan, next generation Barilko fan."

Thirty years Evan's senior, I feel every one of my extra years after picking my way across the muskeg to get here again. My body has become a ledger of recent troubles, and I've spent the past two years as a lab rat. Three colonoscopies, three MRIs, two CT scans, multiple ultrasounds and X-rays, emergency surgery, repeated biopsies, months of anti-inflammatory medications, a bout of steroids, and countless urine, blood, and stool tests. All of it in an attempt to diagnose and treat a mysterious ailment that sprung upon me suddenly just as I was about to turn fifty and has stripped thirty pounds from my already slender frame, leaving me leaner and weaker than I've ever known myself to be.

Yet every ending offers up a new beginning. When my pilgrimage to Barilko is over, I intend to disappear for a while and do what Barilko was blessed to do for so many years. Play hockey. No deadlines, no interviews, no obligations tugging at the edges of every day. Just hockey. I imagine long stretches of unclaimed time and the familiar chill of an arena. There is a grace in the game, a temporary silencing of whatever noise the world places inside our heads. The rink is my shrink, the game my therapy. Out on the ice, chasing a puck beneath bright lights, the body remembers what it can still do, and the mind, for an hour or two, forgets everything else. In chasing the ghosts of Bill Barilko and Henry Hudson into the northern wilderness, I've become a specter myself, a wraithlike resemblance to the man who did this trek not even four years ago. Different season, same result. Still no sign.

"There's also the possibility that somebody came in here with a helicopter or something and took the sign," Chad says, refusing to give up the search.

Could the sign have been poached? It seems too sinister for the story, but the possibility enters in my mind as I stand among these trees for the second time and for the second time see nothing but trees. The wreckage is gone. Barilko and Hudson are gone. Even the decades that separate us from the crash have begun to blur and soften. But the story remains, stubborn and enduring, passed from one generation to the next like an old campfire tale. The sign, along with the puck beneath it, is one of the few physical things connecting the world of myth to an actual place on a map. For someone captivated by the legend, it might've seemed less like a piece of aluminum nailed to a tree than a relic to be pilfered.

Perhaps someone had come looking not for the crash site itself but for a piece of the story they could carry away. The thought feels strangely fitting. For nearly seventy-five years, people have been taking pieces of the story home with them, retelling it in arenas, bars, newspaper columns, songs, and books. Why not a sign? The forest surrendered the wreckage long ago. Maybe, in time, it surrendered the sign as well.

After about an hour of searching, we've all come up empty. As we gather back together, none of us openly admits our collective disappointment. The silence between us says it all.

Of our group, Mark has hunted the hardest, checking and rechecking every clearing, every downed tree, every inch of ground within the vicinity of the coordinates. Yet there isn't a hint of regret on his face. He doffs his bug suit, revealing the Leafs hat and hoodie he's wearing underneath, then reaches into his backpack and pulls out some screws and a screwdriver and a small cardboard-covered package.

"A screwdriver?" I ask. "I'm intrigued."

"What has Fera got up his sleeve?" Steve wonders aloud as Mark rolls up his cuffs.

"It's a three-part series," Mark says. "This is number one."

Mark peels off the cardboard to reveal a small replica of Barilko's banner hanging in the rafters in Toronto.

"The first thing that we're going to do is, Bill is one of the first two Leafs who had their number retired, Ace Bailey being the other one," Mark begins. "With Bill losing his life and this being the location of where it happened, this is the banner, and it's been put together in glass right from the plexiglass for the boards from Scotiabank Arena. So, we'll have a little bit of the old and a little bit of the new as we leave it. I think we'll put it on this young tree here so that way it can grow with the story."

As Mark screws the banner into the tree, Steve turns to Chad and says: "You've gotta mark the latitude and longitude of this spot. This is gonna be the new spot."

"Well, this is pretty much the spot that we had."

Mark has more. He reaches into his backpack again and pulls out a puck.

"We can't do it properly unless we have the actual puck to go with the goal," he says. "I don't think it will ever be a bigger moment than having the actual puck that Bill scored the goal with in 1951."

The puck is a story unto itself. For decades, one of hockey's most coveted relics was believed to rest safely in the possession of the Hockey Hall of Fame. Yet in a modest Hamilton home, another story unfolded in silence. There, on the family mantel, sat a battered black puck that'd landed there after the greatest night in Leafs history, kept not as a museum piece but as a family treasure.

As the Leafs surged across the ice to engulf Barilko after winning the Stanley Cup in 1951, sixteen-year-old Harry Donohue noticed something everyone else had overlooked. The puck still lay undisturbed in the back of the net. He turned to his father, Jeremiah, and asked if he could retrieve it. With his father's nod, and the quiet consent of a rinkside usher, the boy stepped onto the ice, maneuvered through the fading chaos, and lifted the puck from the mesh.

On his way back to his seat, a stranger stopped him and offered $20 for it, a considerable sum in 1951. Harry refused without hesitation.

The following day, his grandfather sought out a local craftsman, who fashioned a simple wooden display case. From then on, the puck occupied a place of honor on the Donohue family's mantel. It was revered, though not untouchable. Harry and his brothers occasionally liberated it from its case to fire slap shots around the basement, blissfully unconcerned that they were playing with a piece of hockey folklore.

Only years later did questions begin to surface about the celebrated puck that the Hall of Fame had in its possession. Photographs and archival film, some of it unseen for decades, supported the stories the Donohues passed from one generation to the next. The footage tells a compelling story. As jubilant Leafs players swarm Barilko, another puck can be seen tumbling onto the ice from somewhere in the stands, perhaps the very one that eventually found its way to the Hall. The accepted tale held that the referee had given a young boy in a wheelchair the game puck, which then ended up in the Hall. But another figure appears in the film: a solitary young man in street clothes, almost certainly Harry, walking purposefully toward the goalmouth.

The Donohue family knew nothing of the Hall's competing claim until 2013, long after both Jeremiah and Harry had passed away. As they began piecing together the evidence, an intriguing detail emerged. The puck in the Hall's collection bore a white manufacturer's stamp identifying it as a Spalding model produced between 1920 and 1942. The Donohue puck tells a different story. Its orange crest marks it as the newly introduced vulcanized Art Ross model, the very puck that entered NHL play in 1950.

"And to top it all off, let's hit a home run here," Mark says, mixing sports metaphors. "Why not reunite Bill with his 1951 Stanley Cup ring as well that he never got to see? Today, we've brought that to pay respects to the area where he lost his life and hope that spiritually we're able to connect with him, knowing that we're going to keep the story alive and make sure it's known for generations to come."

Mark mounts the ring and the puck atop the encased banner, and we all gather around for photos.

"What a brilliant idea, Mark," Steve says. "Well done."

"Hold on. I've got one other thing up my sleeve."

Not done yet, Mark digs into his backpack one last time and pulls out a case of Molson Canadian Cold Shots.

"What is a Canadian icon without a couple of Canadian beers while we're in here," he says. "I couldn't take the big ones, but they're nice and cold, so anyone who wants one I've got eight of them."

"I would, but I'm not allowed," Evan says.

"I'll have one because I'm not flying," Chad says. "Should've brought a two-four."

Mark passes each of us a can, except Evan, and we all briefly go silent as we crack open our beers. We're tired, sweaty, bug-bitten, and slightly disheartened that we've failed to find the sign and the puck. But we're here, together, at the site of one of the greatest stories in Canadian history, a place few have ever been. Here, the legend of Bill Barilko ended and his legacy began.

"Listen, you only live once, and you guys have worked your asses off to get in here," Mark says as we all raise our cans for a toast. "Here's to the hockey hero that lives on through every one of us in a different way. Amen."

"Amen."

Fifty Mission Cap and The (Other) Bill Barilko Song

It's more than a hockey story. It's a Canadian story, a tragedy, really, of someone cut down in his prime. It's as much a story of unfulfilled potential as it is hockey.
—Gord Downie, The Tragically Hip

I don't think this story makes sense anywhere else than in a town like Timmins.
—Charlie Angus, Grievous Angels

THE ANCIENT GREEKS HONORED their heroes in song. Canadians are no different. Reach the pinnacle of our national winter sport, and a player will find himself so honored. From "The Ballad of Wendel Clark Parts I and II," to "Elegy for Gump Worsley," and "Clear the Track, Here Comes [Eddie] Shack," the list of Canadian hockey songs is legion. It is a tribute to Bill Barilko, and the power and complexity of his story, that he's been the subject of not one but two musical tributes. One deals with Barilko the overtime hero and Toronto legend. The other is of the regular guy, the product of hardscrabble Timmins.

I pull into the parking lot of a modest low-rise apartment building tucked into a quiet residential pocket of London, Ontario, and slip into a space beside a black Hyundai Kona sporting vanity plates that read BARILKO5. As I cross the lot, the back door of the building swings open and Darryl Deller appears, greeting me with the easy warmth of someone welcoming an old friend rather than a stranger with a notebook. He's dressed in socks, shorts, a Toronto Maple Leafs cap, and a Barilko T-shirt. What he's wearing, however, is only half the story.

The Tragically Hip is the other.

For Darryl, now fifty-three, the two are impossible to separate. They occupy adjoining territories on his body and in his imagination, echoed in the decor of an apartment that feels like a carefully curated museum of devotion. Every wall, dresser, side table, shelf, and spare corner carries evidence of one passion or the other. There are Hip vinyl records and CDs, commemorative stamps, wine bottles and cider cans, as well as framed posters from the band's headlining appearance at Eden Musicfest in Mosport Park in 1996, their *Long Time Running* DVD, and memorabilia from the *Man Machine Poem* tour, including Darryl's ticket from the London show at Budweiser Gardens on August 8, 2016. Counterpointing these are both Barilko biographies, a miniature Maple Leafs Stanley Cup, a Leafs lighter, a tiny Barilko figurine once tucked into a 1950s Kellogg's cereal box, and several hockey cards of Barilko, including the very card Gord Downie used as inspiration for the lyrics to "Fifty Mission Cap."

"When I heard the song for the first time and the line 'the last goal he ever scored won the Leafs the Cup,' I thought, 'This is incredible,'" Darryl says. "Out of all the hockey players that The Tragically Hip and Gord could have written a song about, they chose Bill Barilko."

Anyone can display their loyalty by wearing a jersey or ordering customized license plates. What distinguishes Darryl is the permanence of his devotion. His fandom isn't just arranged on shelves. It's etched right into skin. It pours from beneath his sleeves in dense, black-and-white designs running from shoulder to wrist, with colorful currents of red and blue mixed in. His arms are a living archive devoted to two lifelong obsessions.

His right arm functions as a kind of tattooed setlist of a Hip show, a visual anthology of his favorite songs. Among them is a derringer, a pirate pistol, and a magnum for "Three Pistols." A fleur-de-lis disappears beneath waves for "New Orleans Is Sinking." A 1960s Chevy commemorates "Locked in the Trunk of a Car," paired with an open padlock above a rendering of his BARILKO5 plates. The Bismarck sinks in a plume of smoke for "Nautical Disaster." And, perhaps most fittingly, are the words "It's a Good Life If You Don't Weaken," Darryl's favorite Hip tune, alongside the distinctive heron from the band's *In Violet Light* album cover.

Darryl's left arm belongs to Barilko. "Bashin' Bill" and "Leafs Win the Cup" appear in blue typewriter font. Barilko's career statistics curl around his likeness. There is Barilko's hockey card, complete with his signature, and a hockey puck nestled beneath his number 5. In one especially clever act of reinvention, Darryl asked his tattoo artist to transform an old barbed-wire tattoo from his youth into a re-creation of Nat Turofsky's celebrated photograph, the strands of wire disappearing seamlessly into the crowd.

And still, he insists, the collection is unfinished.

"I'll never get tired of the story," Darryl says. "That and my fandom for Gord and the band and everything else. Hearing 'Fifty Mission Cap,' and to think that he put lyrics to this somewhat obscure player if you're not in the hockey scene. Like, how many people are listening to that song and don't have a clue?"

Far too many. But the link between Barilko and The Hip is less like a historical reference than a kind of Canadian mythology, where memory and meaning become inseparable. In "Fifty Mission Cap," Barilko becomes a symbol of absence itself, a ghost borne along by the nation's imagination. He exists in that liminal space between fact and legend, where history acquires the texture of folklore, transforming a sports story into something literary and almost metaphysical. Over time, the player and the band have become so intertwined because both speak to the same enduring question: how does a country remember itself? In singing Barilko's name, The Hip did more than preserve a story. They became part of it, until the man, the myth, and the music seemed to emanate from the same distant forest.

The story of the song's creation has something of myth about it as well. By the 1990s, Barilko's story had all but slipped out of the country's collective consciousness. It would've disappeared entirely if not for card number 340 from the 1991–92 Pro Set hockey series.

During a rehearsal in the early 1990s, the band was messing around with a lick that bassist Gord Sinclair had brought in. Downie was at his microphone stand opening packs of Pro Set hockey cards and eating the gum when he pulled out a card of Barilko. Number 340. He flipped it over, read the back of it, and then started singing from what New Brunswick hockey historian James Duplacey had written, eventually "stealing" the lyrics out of the last couple of lines of the description:

> *It was the last goal of Barilko's career. He disappeared that summer on a fishing trip, and the Leafs didn't win another Cup until 1962, the year his body was found.*

With that, "Fifty Mission Cap" was born and the Barilko story was brought back to life.

Released as a single in January 1993 off the band's fourth studio album, *Fully Completely*, the song brought Barilko's name and story to a new generation of Canadians. Four months later, with the Leafs just two wins away from reaching the Stanley Cup Final, The Hip, who were on tour in the United States, sent a letter of support to the Leafs in their quest for that ever-elusive Cup that'd evaded Toronto since they'd last won it in 1967, just five years after Barilko had finally been found. It was posted in the team's dressing room at Maple Leaf Gardens ahead of a critical game five against Wayne Gretzky and the Los Angeles Kings, which the Leafs would win 3–2 in overtime, the same score as game five in the 1951 final:

> *Yo! Mighty Leafs. You guys are looking great. Destiny is with you, and so is The Tragically Hip!!! We've been watching all the games on ESPN and won't go on stage until the final buzzer (we're in Georgia right now). All the way, guys. You can do it! (Bill Barilko told us so.)*

More than thirty years on, the song is still a staple at every Leafs home game. From when it was first released to when the band played it last, the song kept popping up on setlists at many of The Hip's biggest shows. At Massey Hall in Toronto, for the first show of their national tour in support of *Fully Completely* back in late 1992, they opened with "Fifty Mission Cap." When they took to the stage at Maple Leaf Gardens as the headliners for the first time ever, on February 10, 1995, the very arena where Barilko scored his storied overtime Cup-winning goal, the band timed a tribute perfectly. As Downie sang the lyric, "The last goal he ever scored won the Leafs the Cup," a spotlight illuminated Barilko's 1951 championship banner as it swayed gently high above the ice. More than twenty years later, facing down Downie's terminal brain cancer diagnosis, the band opened its nationally televised farewell performance on the CBC with "Fifty Mission Cap."

Yet every time The Hip played the song, from the first time they began jamming it out in the early 1990s to the last time they played it at their final show, on August 20, 2016, the lyric that elicited the most cheers wasn't about Barilko. It was about the Leafs. Always the Leafs.

Just as the goal comes before the goal scorer in Foster Hewitt's classic call of Barilko's 1951 overtime winner, so too in "Fifty Mission Cap" does the championship team trump the champion who won it for them. The nostalgia that the song evokes from Leafs fans isn't for the player. It is for the team, and the bygone glory he represents.

Like every Hip song, "Fifty Mission Cap" has to be heard live to be understood. More than just listened to, it has to be seen and felt.

The first time I heard the song live was Saturday, July 24, 1993, when The Hip's cross-country summer festival Another Roadside Attraction rolled into Markham Fairgrounds, just north of Toronto. The band had released *Fully Completely* on October 6, 1992, less than two weeks before the Leafs officially retired Barilko's number 5 in a ceremony at Maple Leaf Gardens, and they'd been touring in support of the album.

Three songs into their headlining set, Downie stepped to the mic to introduce their next song.

"We'd like to do a song about nationalism gone astray," he said. "This is called 'Flag on Your Knapsack.'"

As the band launched into "Fifty Mission Cap," the lights went up and the crowd of sixty thousand surged forward, while Downie feigned fumbling with the mic as the band repeated the song's signature riff until he started singing Barilko's name.

More than forty years after his goal and more than thirty after his body was discovered, Barilko was being cheered again.

There is nothing delicate about "Fifty Mission Cap." It is a story half-told, half-sung, carried on instruments that seem less arranged than rushing forward together. The song arrives already in motion, the door already ajar, with an invitation to enter and join in. From the first note, the groove is immediately in place, as if it were always already there and we've simply arrived late to something significant.

The verse unfolds like newspaper clippings of Barilko's life, half-lost to time. It's always been labeled a hockey song, but it isn't even half so. Only here does Downie sing about Barilko. Even then, he doesn't mention the plane, the crash, or his death (certainly nothing of Henry Hudson), nor anything of Barilko's career beyond him scoring his overtime goal. Downie reverses the order of the story, moving from tragedy to triumph and back again. His voice bends around the phrasing, chasing a tale always out of reach. He sings like a man who knows that telling the story is the only way to keep it alive.

When the bridge is reached, the story is suspended and the hockey card he found it on is tucked into a cap that represents having flown fifty wartime flights. As the chorus arrives, the band tightens just enough to hold the weight of the refrain, so seemingly at odds with the verses, as the novice pilot narrator crushes his cap in the manner of a grizzled airman to make himself appear authentic, much like a rookie seeking stitches and scars to look like a seasoned veteran on the ice.

Downie isn't done with the story. He brings it back to Barilko, repeating his name like a talisman against forgetting. The second time through, as the verse is repeated nearly word for word, the background vocals hover like a distant witness, shadows of the lead voice, interjecting crucial details and bringing the thirty-three words about Barilko up to forty. Had Downie, who'd done a deep dive into the story in the bowels of the Toronto Reference Library, wanted to say more, or felt the song should tell more of the story, he could've done so the second time around.

The song doesn't resolve so much as recede. The instruments drift back into that same steady pulse as the lead guitar, spare and searching until then, steps into the spotlight and continues the story. The legend is left unfinished. It is up to the listener to learn more. There is no closure, just a sense of something carried forward.

Later on in the show at Markham Fairgrounds, during a Rob Baker guitar solo, Downie acted out another hockey metaphor when a shirtless fan jumped onto the stage, somehow managed to escape the gauntlet of onrushing security guards, slapped Downie on the back, leaped back into the crowd, and then disappeared into the pulsating mosh pit. Perhaps Downie was just channeling his inner Barilko, who had a well-earned reputation for always getting a piece of his man. Had Barilko been at the mic, the fan would've ended up Barilkoed for having the temerity to touch him. Dismayed that he hadn't taken the fan down himself, Downie walked over to the left side of the stage, dragging the microphone stand along with him, and began talking and pointing toward that side of the crowd.

"You folks all right down there? When he jumped in, anyone get hurt? Everyone's okay?" he inquired calmly of the fans there before elevating his voice, like Foster Hewitt before a goal.

"I knew I should've tripped him when I saw him running across the stage. I knew I should've taken care of him. I knew I should've taken him down. I should've done it. And I'm sorry. It was my responsibility. He was *my man*!"

As anyone who's looked into the life of Bill Barilko knows, there is an ordinary man behind the myth. A man who liked to fish, who grew up playing hockey on frozen ponds, and who might well have wound up underground in the darkened mines of Timmins instead of under the bright lights of Toronto.

In downtown Toronto, the bar where The Hip were discovered in the 1980s by MCA Records executive Bruce Dickinson looks exactly the way it ought to look. Some places improve themselves into irrelevance. The Horseshoe Tavern has survived by remaining itself. I can feel the history in the building before I even step inside the doors of the city's legendary live music venue. Originally a haunt of biker gangs, the Horseshoe has hosted the likes of The Rolling Stones, The Ramones, The Police, The Talking Heads, and practically every Canadian act that ever mattered, from Bryan Adams to Blue Rodeo to The Hip.

Inside, the first thing I see is a Toronto Maple Leafs decal behind the heavily be-decaled bar to my left. The place is cool and dim. I'm hit with the smell of beer taps, old wood, fryer grease, and amplifier dust, the smells of every proper music venue in the country. Afternoon sunlight leaks through the windows in long amber strips as a heavily inebriated patron at the bar shuffles chairs around at the front. Sunday crowds at the Horseshoe are different from those at nighttime shows. People are less armored. Nobody pretends to be younger or cooler than they are. Just people coming honestly to hear honest songs.

I carry on past the internal A&W pickup window by the bar and then, behind the pool table, the old Triumph Tiger motorcycle that leads to the ticket-only concert area. I step onto the Horseshoe's fabled checkerboard floor and take in the afternoon scene.

The exit signs shine bright in the darkened room. Near the merchandise table, leading to the washrooms downstairs, hangs a framed Ottawa Senators jersey in honor of the late Dave "Bookie" Bookman, a radio and concert host, and rabid Senators fan, who sank his soul into Canada's indie-rock music scene. At the back, the stage gleams with its red and sparkly gold backdrop. A handful of people linger on the dance floor, moving from group to group and conversation to conversation. But most people are sitting down, waiting for the show to begin.

The seats are all taken, so I find a place to stand opposite the bar and look around. The crowd skews older this Sunday afternoon. Gray-haired men and women, some in leather jackets softened by decades of wear, others with a cane or walker at hand. The room hums with low conversation punctuated by the clunk of pint glasses touching wood.

Eventually, the lights dim slightly and the Grievous Angels walk onto the stage to warm applause. Charlie Angus steps to the mic beneath the glow of the stage lights looking like a man who's wandered out of another decade and refused every invitation to leave it behind. He has on a black blazer, the kind of jacket that carries the memory of cigarette smoke, union halls, and long winter tours through mining towns. Beneath it, his shirt blazes a reckless pink, bright and unapologetic, like the last flare of sunset over dirty snowbanks. A dark gray fedora sits low on his head, tilted with the weary confidence of someone who's spent half his life leaning into microphones and the other half arguing with the world. His sunburst lacquer guitar glows amber and tobacco-brown in the dimly lit room. There is nothing polished about him, nothing curated for nostalgia. He looks instead like the last believer in some ragged gospel of barroom rock and prairie politics, a man dressed for the hard-earned right to keep singing.

The Grievous Angels have brought a little Northern Ontario with them to the center of downtown Toronto, including, as befits the former member of parliament for Timmins–James Bay, some of Charlie's NDP politics. The band opens with a few roots-rock numbers that roll warmly through the room. There are songs about resistance and revolution, highways and mining. People nod along into their drinks and tap their feet in rhythm to the music. I listen patiently and attentively as the band powers through their setlist, but I am here for only one song.

As a kid in Timmins, Charlie grew up listening to stories his father told him about his high school friend Bill. They were happy stories of best friends and the shenanigans they got up to as teenage boys. There were also the stories about his friend leaving Timmins to play hockey in Hollywood, of all places, then getting the call-up to Toronto to play for the Maple Leafs, and the overtime goal that made him famous and put Timmins forever on the map of hockey history.

"I always felt that this was our story," Charlie had said when we met a few days before the gig. "You had to know the Bill Barilko story. I didn't even know there was a national significance to it. We used to hear the stories of Bill Barilko. He and my dad went to Central Public School together. He and Bill were really good friends. Bill was a big guy, good-looking guy, tough guy. But my dad never talked about the tragedy. He talked about Bill full of life and fun. My dad didn't like the darker part of the story. He used to talk about them wrestling in the halls at Central Public and banging down the lockers, because my dad was a big guy and Bill was a big boy too. They were all very physical back then. They were physical kids, they liked to fight, they played sports. Bill was such a dynamic character in our memory."

In the early 1990s, perhaps looking back on his childhood with the distance of the years, Charlie wrote a song inspired by the stories his dad used to tell him about his buddy Bill. He brought it to a good friend of his who was also in the music industry. Charlie told him he'd just written a song about Bill Barilko, the quintessential Canadian story. Charlie's pal was also friends with The Hip.

"He goes, 'Haven't you heard the new Tragically Hip record that just came out?'" Charlie recalled his friend saying. "I said, 'No, no, why?' He goes, 'I don't want to break your heart, but Gord Downie beat you to the Bill Barilko song.' And I was like, 'He's a Boston Bruins fan. What's he doing singing about Bill Barilko?' So every time someone talks about the Bill Barilko song, it's The Tragically Hip. But you know what, I don't mind. If I'm going to lose out to anybody in the big leagues, I can afford losing to The Hip. I love The Hip and I love the song, but I didn't love the song in the sense that, to me, it wasn't a hockey card. It was a whole fabric of life. It was a way of life. It was a people. I knew these people through the fabric of story. But I mean, am I going to argue with Gord Downie? No."

Having been scooped by The Hip, the Grievous Angels didn't end up releasing "The Bill Barilko Song" until four years later, in 1996, as part of their fourth album, *Waiting for the Cage*. Over time, the song had slipped off the band's setlists, until it'd been years since they'd last played it live. But with the seventy-fifth anniversary approaching, and a gig lined up in the city where Barilko scored his overtime goal, the band decided it was time to dust it off for their show on this late-spring Sunday afternoon at the Horseshoe.

Finally, four songs deep into their second set, Charlie introduces it.

"We're going to take you back up to Northern Ontario now," he tells the crowd. "In the 1940s, you had a choice: you either followed your father underground into the mines or you learned to be really good at hockey and hope to play for the Toronto Maple Leafs. I wrote this song at the same time The Tragically Hip released 'Fifty Mission Cap,' which is a little like being Jimmy of Nazareth. This is called 'The Bill Barilko Song.'"

Immediate recognition spreads through the Horseshoe like a current running through wire. "The Bill Barilko Song" doesn't catapult the listener into the story like "Fifty Mission Cap." It unfolds gently, without ceremony. The instruments arrive already in place, as if they've always been here. There is no sharp edge to mark the beginning, only the gradual sense of a narrative taking shape. Charlie's vocals have a homespun quality to them, something worn but honest, having lived with this story for years.

Plainspoken and unadorned, his words carry the unmistakable cadence of a story passed down from father to son:

The sun is on the McIntyre
The kids are at the rink
Yesterday ain't so far as I used to think
Bill, sometimes I think of you
You wear the white and blue
When every dream and glory and all the dreams came true

Neither showy nor insistent, Charlie simply tells the story, trusting that the truth of it is enough. The verses move steadily as the story unfolds, each one another turn of the page, another piece of the past laid bare.

No shortage of Cinderellas in any mining town
All dream of coming back home wearing a golden crown
Bill, you wore the white and blue, always looked so grand
Came back home in '51, biggest hero in the land

The choruses, when they arrive, feel less like a release and more like a gathering of voices, and an invitation to sing along:

Bashin' Bill, won't you come on home
Sha la la la la, la la la la la, la la la la la la la
The world keeps on changing
We all grow old but you
Sha la la la la, la la la la la, oh Bill I think of you

As the song drifts to its end, it finishes without a firm resolution, fading out in mystery. It leaves behind the sense that the story isn't over. It's been passed along, carried forward in the telling, in the singing, as steady and enduring as the memory of Barilko himself:

I got a sweater with a number five
It's never been worn, you know
The search planes never had much luck in North Ontario

Charlie has lived with the Barilko story from the age of six, when his father began taking him every year to Timmins Memorial Cemetery, where his friend was buried. It is a ritual Charlie has continued himself into his sixties. After the tour is over, and Charlie heads back home to Northern Ontario, he'll make his annual pilgrimage to Barilko's gravesite and revisit all the stories, both triumphant and tragic, that led his father's friend there so young, and reflect on the legend that surrounds him.

"I don't know what other people think of the song, but for us the song is a song of Canada, the song of a moment, and a song of hockey," Charlie said. "Heck, the Leafs have sucked for so long, at least we've got some good legends and lore to listen to."

Call to the Hall

This I know: as goes Barilko, so go the Leafs.
—King Clancy, honored member of the Hockey Hall of Fame

I CLIMB THE WOODEN STAIRCASE with a private anticipation that feels something akin to game day. When I reach the top, the space opens above me in solemn grandeur, cathedral-like and hallowed, crowned by a stained-glass dome. This vast chamber was once the central banking hall of a Victorian palace of commerce. Now, it is a house of religion. Around me, venerable trophies reflect the colored light: the Hart, the Rocket Richard, the Norris, the Vezina, the Calder, the Lady Byng. At the center of the hall is the holy chalice itself. All of hockey history gravitates toward it. People gather around it instinctively, their movements slowing, their voices dropping. Some take photographs. Others simply stand, hands clasped or tucked into pockets, uncertain whether reverence requires stillness or motion. I circle it once, then again. The names engraved along its bands blur into a continuous narrative. Here is victory, repeated yet never diminished. I wonder about the hands that've lifted it, the brief moment when, however heavy it is, it felt weightless for its winners.

Standing in front of the Stanley Cup, in the Great Hall at the Hockey Hall of Fame, among all this silver and reverence, my thoughts turn to Bill Barilko. To me, his absence looms larger than any victory preserved here. Of all the players who've touched the Cup in triumph, no one in the history of the NHL has won it more often over fewer years than Barilko. Yet he isn't commemorated here, and likely never will be. He played just four years, two months, and fifteen days in the NHL over five seasons in the league, not nearly enough, according to most, for him to be recognized as among the game's greatest players.

Greatness. Sometimes it hits you like a puck in the face. Maurice Richard, Gordie Howe, Bobby Orr, Wayne Gretzky, Mario Lemieux, these were players who revolutionized the game. But small would be the Hall if only the greatest of the greatest were granted entry. For most of the players who reside here, their greatness was less obvious, and the consensus about it emerged more subtly, through debate or with the passage of time. Sometimes, as in Barilko's case, it's been missed entirely.

Farther out from the Cup, past the other trophies, arrayed in quiet, ordered dignity, the plaques of the inducted look back at me in stillness, their faces fixed at the age of victory. Many of Barilko's teammates are here: Turk Broda, Ted Kennedy, Max Bentley, and Howie Meeker among them. Every one of them would've said, indeed did say, that Barilko belongs here too. I decide to walk around to ask each of them why.

I step first to Broda, the stout yet steady goaltender who stood behind Barilko for those five glorious seasons. In 1967, fifteen years after he'd retired, Broda was asked on *Hockey Night in Canada* to name the best defenseman who ever played in front of him. Even though Broda, who spent his entire career with the Toronto Maple Leafs, had played behind such greats as Hap Day, King Clancy, Red Horner, Babe Pratt, and Fern Flaman, each one a Hall of Fame defenseman, he named none of them.

"Bill Barilko," Broda said unequivocally.

I turn next to Kennedy, the courageous captain who led Barilko and the rest of the Maple Leafs and shared in that last Stanley Cup triumph in 1951 before tragedy changed everything. In 1969, long after he'd retired from playing, Kennedy was in the mix for the vacant head coaching job of the Leafs. He didn't get the gig, but in the running he was asked to name his all-Leafs team of the previous twenty-five years. Up front, he selected Syl Apps between wingers Sweeney Schriner and George Armstrong. In goal, he chose Broda. On defense, he went with Jimmy Thomson. And Barilko.

"Barilko would have become an all-star in my opinion," Kennedy said, "if he had not lost his life in an offseason plane crash."

Then there is Bentley, whose offensive brilliance complemented the rugged resilience Barilko brought to the blueline, their styles different but cut from the same championship cloth.

"When Bill was on the ice, he was fearless," Bentley said. "If the accident hadn't happened, he would've been one of the greatest."

Finally, I turn to Meeker, a teammate who skated alongside Barilko and then later, in the broadcast booth, became one of the voices who kept those memories alive long after the silence had settled.

"He was a heck of a hockey player," Meeker said. "He would have been a Hall of Famer. There's no doubt in my mind."

As I stand here beneath the dome, I feel how the past in this room isn't settled at all, but waiting, as it always has, for someone missing, for a player who belongs alongside his teammates, along with the greatest to have ever played the game.

Had his career continued, it is easy to imagine Barilko becoming one of the defining defensemen of the 1950s, easily surpassing the individual accomplishments of his remarkable early years and continuing the Leafs' dominance of the 1940s into the next decade. It is no coincidence that the Leafs didn't win another Stanley Cup for eleven years after his disappearance. Throughout the rest of the 1950s, when Barilko would've been in his prime, they finished no higher than third place, missed the playoffs three times, and didn't even win another playoff series for eight years. Because Barilko was such a physical force defensively, Smythe, Day, and Primeau all overlooked his obvious offensive instincts and talent, as have hockey historians since. He was the engine that powered the Leafs, their best rear guard on a rear wheel–drive team. The great King Clancy, one of the NHL's best defensemen of the 1920s and '30s, saw this as a league referee after his playing days when he concluded, rightly, "As goes Barilko, so go the Leafs." He understood it himself in his three years as coach in the mid-1950s when, without Barilko, the Leafs finished no higher than third place, lost in the semifinals each year, and won only two out of fourteen playoff games.

Barilko's trajectory pointed unmistakably upward, on a career that would've taken him here, into the Great Hall. Few dispute this. But a player must be evaluated for what he did, not what he was likely to do. Barilko simply didn't live long enough to play long enough, his naysayers say, and that is where the debate usually ends.

In June 2005, the Hockey Hall of Fame tabled its decisive judgment when the selection committee reviewed a proposal brought by Dr. John Shaw, who was part of a group that had gathered ten thousand signatures in support of getting Barilko inducted. It was quietly and swiftly rejected.

The case against Barilko always comes down to longevity and statistics: 26 goals and 36 assists for 62 points in 252 games, along with 456 penalty minutes, during the regular season; and 5 goals and 7 assists for 12 points in 47 games, with 104 penalty minutes, in the playoffs. These simple stats are used to prove that his production doesn't merit induction.

To counter this argument, people who believe Barilko belongs in the Hall inevitably turn to the overtime goal, the mystery, the story that still echoes through hockey history. The move is understandable but misguided. It is an appeal to emotion when a deeper dive into statistics would meet Barilko's detractors where they're at and steelman the case for his induction. Strip away the legend, and the numbers alone tell a story that is even more compelling.

From his first game, February 6, 1947, to his last, April 21, 1951, Barilko was the NHL's second-highest goal-scoring defensemen, regular season and playoffs combined, behind only the great Red Kelly, who was basically the Bobby Orr of Barilko's era. Take any five-year period in NHL history from 1917 to 2000, and nearly three-quarters of the thirty-six defensemen who finished second in goals are in the Hockey Hall of Fame. This puts Barilko in an elite tier of defensemen alongside the likes of Sprague Cleghorn, Eddie Shore, Pierre Pilote, Brad Park, Denis Potvin, Ray Bourque, Paul Coffey, Al MacInnis, and Nicklas Lidström. Never much of a playmaker, Barilko was instead near the top in virtually every single goal-scoring statistic among defensemen in the regular season during his career: tied for third in goals (26), tied for fourth in even-strength goals (20), tied for ninth in power-play goals (3), tied for first in shorthanded goals (3), and tied for eleventh in game-winning goals (2). In the playoffs, he ranked even higher: tied for second in goals (5), tied for second in even-strength goals (4), tied for second in power-play goals (1), and second in game-winning goals (2).

If the numbers look small, it is because they were for every defenseman of his time. That was the world Barilko played in, an era when defensemen, even the most offensively gifted of them, were told to defend first and score, well, never. No defenseman, except for Kelly, who was converted into a forward later in his career, was ever given the green light to go on offense. Scoring was solely for forwards. Defensemen were straitjacketed, imprisoned within an area of the ice that extended from the boards behind their own net to the offensive blue line. No farther. Those who dared to cross this imaginary line installed by the game's old-school, out-of-touch executives and coaches were browbeaten, suspended, or, in the case of Barilko, fined.

"In our day, it was taboo for defensemen to get to the top of the circle, even," Meeker said. "That was going in deep, the top of the circle."

Despite these restrictions, Barilko made his mark on NHL history in his short time in the league. When compared with the best defensemen of his era, his rightful place among the game's greats becomes clear.

Over Barilko's career, a total of seventy-three defensemen played at least one game in the NHL. Nine of them would go on to the Hockey Hall of Fame: Jack Stewart, Butch Bouchard, Ken Reardon, Red Kelly, Bill Gadsby, Doug Harvey, Bill Quackenbush, Allan Stanley, and Fern Flaman. (Marcel Pronovost and Tim Horton would as well, but Pronovost's career overlapped Barilko's for only 52 games and Horton's for just two.) While he was in the league, Barilko scored more goals than Quackenbush, Gadsby, Harvey, Bouchard, Stanley, Flaman, Reardon, and Stewart, all of whom were either the same age or older. Only Kelly had more goals, and even then Barilko matched him in both goals and points in the playoffs, when the games mattered most and Barilko was at his best. Barilko also had more assists than Bouchard, Flaman, and Stanley, and more points than the three of them plus Stewart. Barilko accumulated all of his totals before the end of the first month after his twenty-fourth birthday, and he did so despite being given limited power-play time, rarely seeing top-pair minutes, and starting most of his shifts in the defensive zone, because his coaches pigeonholed him as purely a defensive defenseman.

Goals-per-game tell a similar story. Over his time in the league, Barilko ranked third in the regular season and fourth in the playoffs among all defensemen, more than Harvey, Quackenbush, Flaman, Bouchard, Stanley, Reardon, and Stewart. The disparity becomes even greater when expanded to career averages. Barilko's regular season average (0.103) dwarfed the marks of all seven of those Hall of Famers, and his playoff average (0.106) even more so.

Barilko accomplished all of this while earning the reputation as the roughest, toughest, and hardest-hitting defenseman in the league, ranking fourth overall in penalty minutes during the regular season (456) and first during the postseason (104).

Yet dig even deeper into Barilko's numbers and something happens. A statistical trail emerges that anyone willing to look beyond basic stats can follow, one that leads straight to the Hockey Hall of Fame alongside his contemporaries.

Traditional Hall of Fame arguments lean on standard career totals: how long a player lasted, how many goals they scored, how many points they piled up over time. But there are newer and better ways of looking at the game, numbers pulled together out of traditional statistics that reveal how much a player helped his team win while he was on the ice.

"Adjusted goals created" is an estimate of how many goals a player is truly responsible for creating, not just scoring. It takes their goals and assists, then adjusts for things like team scoring levels and era so that players can be compared fairly across different seasons. In simple terms, it reveals how much offense a player actually generated for his team.

"Point shares" measures how many of a team's points in the standings (in Barilko's era, that meant wins and ties) a player contributed. Broken down into "offensive point shares," "defensive point shares," and "total point shares," it divides credit among players based on their offense and defense, giving a rough idea of their overall value. In essence, it shows how many points a team earns because of a specific player.

By these four metrics, Barilko shines. When adjusted to an 82-game schedule, the baseline for these comparisons, Bariko's career averages match or even exceed those of every other top defenseman from his era, both offensively and defensively.

Take Stewart, who was known for his toughness and shutdown ability. He played twelve seasons in the NHL, most of them with the Detroit Red Wings, including all five that Barilko was in the league. Barilko didn't just match him; he outperformed him. Offensively, Barilko generated over three times the offensive impact and was stronger defensively, where Stewart earned his reputation and built his case for induction. In fact, Barilko surpassed Stewart in all four adjusted metrics over their respective careers: adjusted goals created (10.5 to 8.0), offensive point shares (1.4 to 0.4), defensive point shares (6.0 to 5.5), and total point shares (7.5 to 6.0). Although Stewart scored five more goals than Barilko did over his career, it took him 346 more games to do so. Barilko wasn't just comparable; he was the more complete player.

Reardon is another Hall of Famer whose career is often praised for its consistency and defensive acumen. Of all nine Hall of Fame defensemen, he is perhaps closest in comparison to Barilko. He played seven seasons, all with the Montreal Canadiens, including four of the five that Barilko was in the league. Reardon piled up more assists and points over his career, but Barilko scored three more goals despite playing 84 fewer games. Zoom in on how much the two players contributed in a typical season and Barilko holds his own, either equaling or coming just shy of Reardon in adjusted goals created (13.2 to 10.5), offensive point shares (1.8 to 1.4), defensive point shares (6.0 to 6.0), and point shares (7.8 to 7.5). Like Reardon, Barilko's impact wasn't about racking up numbers over a long career. It was about how effective he was every time he stepped on the ice.

Expand the comparison, and the same pattern repeats itself.

Career-wise, Barilko's adjusted goals created (10.5) is better than Bouchard's (8.6); his offensive points shares (1.4) are higher than Bouchard's (0.7); his defensive points shares (6.0) are higher than Harvey's (5.9), Quackenbush's (5.2), Stanley's (4.9), Kelly's (4.4), and Gadsby's (3.5); his total points shares (7.5) are higher than Quackenbush's (7.3), Bouchard's (7.2), Stanley's (6.8), and Gadsby's (6.6); and he surpasses Flaman in all four categories. Even when broken down season by season, from 1946–47 to 1950–51, Barilko repeatedly topped Bouchard, Flaman, Gadsby, Stanley, and Stewart across all four categories, and sometimes even Harvey and Quackenbush.

By the game's greatest accomplishment, Barilko also bests every Hall of Fame defenseman from his five seasons in the league. And it isn't even close. He won the Stanley Cup the same number of times as Stewart, Reardon, Flaman, Gadsby, and Quackenbush did. Combined. Like Barilko, Stanley and Bouchard each won the Cup four times, but they needed twenty-one and fifteen seasons to do so. Barilko just five. Only Kelly and Harvey went on to win the Stanley Cup more often than Barilko did. Kelly won it eight times in nineteen seasons, while Harvey won six in fifteen.

When viewed comprehensively, the statistical argument against Barilko just doesn't hold up. In fact, it stacks up in favor of Barilko.

What about the fact that he never won any individual awards? Well, there were almost none for him to win. With competition like Howe, Richard, Milt Schmidt, and Sid Abel, Barilko was never going to win the Hart Trophy as the league's most valuable player, and he most certainly wasn't going to win the Lady Byng Trophy as the league's most sportsmanlike player. The James Norris Trophy for the league's best defenseman wasn't awarded until the 1953–54 season, and it took until the 1964–65 season for the Conn Smythe Trophy to be handed out to the playoff MVP, an honor Barilko would've likely won in 1950–51. Barilko was a beast throughout those entire playoffs, driving the play for the Leafs offensively while shutting it down defensively. Of the thirty goals the Leafs scored that postseason, he was on the ice for seventeen of them; of the fifteen the Leafs gave up, he was on the receiving end of only four. With three goals and five points in twelve games, all of them at even-strength, he led all defensemen in scoring and, of course, scored the Stanley Cup overtime winner.

The only award Barilko actually had an opportunity to win was the Calder Trophy for the league's best rookie. He would've won it had he played a full season in 1946–47, when he led not only all rookie defensemen but all NHL defensemen in points per game (0.56). Even then, no defenseman in the league was ever really given a chance to win the award. In the first thirty years that the Calder Trophy was handed out, not one defenseman ever won it. It wasn't until 1962–63 that it was finally given to a defenseman, the Leafs' twenty-six-year-old Kent Douglas.

Another knock against Barilko is that he was never named a first-team or second-team all-star. The NHL began naming its first-team and second-team all-stars (not to be confused with players in all-star games) at all six positions in the 1930–31 season. In the first twenty-one years of these honors, through Barilko's last season, there were eighty-four all-star nods for defensemen. Only seven of them were given to players under twenty-five years old. In what was an old boys' network of the time, young defensemen were repeatedly passed over in favor of veterans, even though the average age league-wide was around twenty-five.

"If Barilko hadn't died, but kept on playing and acquired the mental finesse that comes with it," Meeker said, "I can safely say that Bill would've been a first-team all-star from the ages of twenty-seven to thirty-two."

Yet another knock on Barilko is that he simply didn't play long enough in the NHL to merit consideration. If so, then neither did Reardon, who got into the Hockey Hall of Fame playing only 84 more games than Barilko did. That equates to just one more regular season in today's NHL. If brevity is a knock on Barilko, then it should've been against Reardon too.

Then there is this: of all NHL players to win the Stanley Cup at least four times, Barilko has the highest cups-to-seasons ratio (eighty percent) in league history, and the great Henri Richard is the only player to win the Cup more times before the age of twenty-five.

Put it all together, and Barilko's case is impossible to ignore. He wasn't a memorable figure just because of one famous goal or the tragic ending. He was, statistically, one of the best defensemen of his time. In fact, aside from the incomparable Kelly, who was really a forward disguised as a defenseman, Barilko was the NHL's greatest goal-scoring defenseman from the day he entered the league to the day he departed it. If the Hockey Hall of Fame is meant to recognize players who truly made an impact, then the numbers, quietly but convincingly, make the case that Barilko belongs in the Great Hall alongside his teammates. Statistics are all that need to be said. No emotional appeal to the story is needed.

When I finally turn toward the exit, the light shifts again. I glance back once more, not out of obligation but because something in me has been altered, subtly but undeniably. The game, I realize, isn't only what happens on the ice. It is also what endures after the final whistle, what is carried forward in stories and in the places where they happened and in the objects left behind. From Timmins to Hollywood to, triumphantly,

Toronto, and then finally, tragically, the forbidding forest of Northern Ontario, Barilko left behind a legacy that has continued long after he left this world. I've followed the trail he blazed so bright: from a flagship grocery store in Toronto; to his home arena and the cemetery where he rests in Timmins; to a park and a resort in sunny Southern California, where he took Hollywood by storm; to a pair of university rinks, an NHL arena, a law office, and a railway underpass in Toronto; to the lake he departed from on his fishing trip and never returned; to the two towns on the east coast of James Bay, where he was last seen alive; to the Hudson Plain in Northern Ontario, where he perished in the plane crash; and to the Canadian musicians who've eulogized him in song. Along the way, I've found his story archived in the newspapers and periodicals of his day, among everyday groceries, recorded on banners, captured in photographs, remembered in plaques, portrayed in posters, honored in elaborate displays, artwork, and murals, exulted in song, inked on the arms of a superfan, and embodied in the wreckage of the plane that carried him to the other side.

Everywhere I've been, I've found his story. Except here, the one place that matters most. His boss and coaches are all here, as are many of his teammates. May one day he join them, in the quiet reverence of a place that refuses to let players like him and stories like his fade.

Bill Barilko belongs in the Hockey Hall of Fame for everything he accomplished and represents in his short career. From his first NHL game to the last goal he ever scored.

EPILOGUE

Frozen in Time

If Bill Barilko was a New York Yankee, there would've been movies made about him. If he was a Dallas Cowboy, movies would've been made about him. If he was a member of the Los Angeles Lakers, there would've been movies made about him. But he was Canadian, and we're negligent in that respect. We just don't hold our myths out as widely as we should, and I think shame on us that we don't.
—Kevin Vincent, Hudson–Barilko Recovery Project

THE MOMENT WAS CAUGHT on camera. Fifteen minutes into a twenty-two-minute appearance on *The Agenda*, TVO's long-running current affairs program, I'd just finished speaking about the greatest goal ever scored in the long and storied history of the Toronto Maple Leafs and about the curious lack of cinematic recognition afforded the man who scored it. Across the desk, host Steve Paikin regarded me with a look that suggested he was entertaining a private thought. A smile crept across his face. Then, without waiting for the cameras to stop rolling, he said:

"Ronnie, I got an idea. You and I are gonna have a chat after we finish this interview. I have an idea. You're gonna like it. I got an idea. Stand by."

I had no idea what he was talking about. The remark landed so lightly that I paid it little mind. The interview ended. The studio lights remained bright as the producers stepped forward to remove our microphones. Only then did Steve rise from behind his desk and walk toward me, the same lightbulb smile still on his face.

"Ronnie," he said, "let's do it."

I stared at him blankly.

We'd never met before that day. Yet we shared instincts as Canadian journalists with a passion for sports: a love of the game, a fascination with the story, a deep appreciation for our country, and a moral compass for bringing buried mysteries into the light. Whatever Steve was proposing, I was already all in before I knew what it was.

"All right," I said. "Let's do it. What are we doing?"

In hindsight, the answer seems obvious. The script was already there, waiting to be written.

There are stories that belong to a country the way rivers belong to a landscape. They run across the surface, shaping a nation's history whether people notice them or not. Barilko's is one of them.

The story possesses all the elements that writers spend lifetimes inventing: victory, disappearance, mystery, longing, coincidence, and fate. It begins, as all good legends do, with triumph, and ends where all life leads, to tragedy. One moment, he is a hero holding a trophy above his head. The next he is a question mark suspended over the country.

Until Steve's sudden flash of inspiration in that television studio, the thought of returning to the crash site had never crossed my mind. I'd already made my pilgrimage. I'd paid my respects to Bill Barilko and Henry Hudson and done what I could to honor their memory.

But stories have a way of calling us back.

The bush, vast and silent, reached out and pulled me in once more. Somewhere deep down, I understood that it wouldn't release me until the story had been told in full. Not just in a book, but on film. It demanded a documentary worthy of the man, the mystery, and the enduring power of both.

That realization set in motion more than a year of meetings, fundraising pitches, false starts, and long stretches of hurry-up-and-wait. Steve and I searched for investors who believed in the project and a production company willing to share our vision. Doors opened. Others closed. Progress arrived in fits and starts. After one poignant rejection, I wondered whether it would ever happen at all.

Eventually, the pieces came together. The financing was secured. The filmmaker was found. All that remained was a title:

Frozen in Time: The Bill Barilko Story

By the time I returned to the Northern Ontario wilderness with Steve, we were far from alone when we hiked to the crash site with our guide Chad Calaiezzi, pilot Evan Green, and Maple Leafs superfan Mark Fera, aka "That Toronto Maple Leafs Guy." With us stood the team that made the journey possible. Producer Barry Avrich oversaw the shoot. Director of photography Ken Ng and first assistant cameraman Chris Monette captured every step on film, while Stephen Dranitsaris worked the sound. Back in Toronto, producer Mark Selby kept the production running behind the scenes, while line producer Melissa Coghlan orchestrated the countless details required to get us all from Toronto to Timmins and then on to the crash site.

"I know you and I are having no problem with this at all," Steve had said to Chad partway through the trek to the site. "But is it more difficult when you have to drag the asses of a bunch of producers who don't know what they're doing?"

"Uh, I think that goes without saying, doesn't it?" Chad replied with a hearty laugh. "No doubt about it, we'd be there already."

Like all successful expeditions, it was never the work of one person. It was a collective effort, a group of people united by a belief that some stories deserve to be pursued to the very place where history and myth become indistinguishable.

The Bill Barilko story lacks neither grandeur, nor sorrow, but it does ask questions that make the country uncomfortable. It issues a direct encounter with tragedy and demands an account of how we would respond to it, whether we would wither in the face of fate or fashion meaning out of the resulting wreckage. It asks that age-old question of whether it is better to burn bright or fade away. Canada prefers modesty to monument, understatement to declaration. To have left such a story untold in the language of film for so long is to confess a certain uncertainty about ourselves, a fear of the very land we live upon, and a hesitation before the idea that a Canadian life is large enough to occupy the dimensions of tragedy.

For too long, Barilko's empty seat in the theater of Canadian film left a quiet vacancy in the national consciousness. The story is Canadian, sure, but there is something universal about it. It begs to be shared with the world. Bill Barilko's story has been sung, heard, listened to, and written about. Now, it can finally be seen too.

Sources

Newspapers, periodicals, and online archives were the main sources for the book: *Canadian Press*, *Cochrane Northland Post*, (Timmins) *Daily Press*, *Financial Post*, (Montreal) *Gazette*, *Globe and Mail*, *Los Angeles Evening Citizen News*, *Los Angeles Times*, *Maclean's*, *Maple Leaf Gardens Official Programme and Sports Magazine*, *National Post*, NHL.com, *North Bay Nugget*, *Ottawa Citizen*, *Outdoor Canada*, *Star Weekly*, (Toronto) *Telegram*, *The Hockey News*, *Toronto Star*, and *Toronto Sun*.

All quotes by and about Bill Barilko came from their crackerjack writers and reporters, both past and present: Red Burnett, Gordon Campbell, Dink Carroll, James Christie, Don Delaplante, Rick Drennan, Braven Dyer, Chloé Fedio, Stan Fischler, Ed Fitkin, Denis Grayhurst, Bob Hesketh, Bobby Hewitson, Lance Hornby, Andy Lytle, Craig MacInnis, Gerry McAuliffe, Bob McKenzie, Allan Nickleson, Joe O'Connor, Ken Pagan, Bob Pennington, Joe Perlove, Wayne Scanlan, Jim Vipond, Gord Walker, Ben Ward, Charles Wilkins, Kenneth R. Wilson, and Peter Worthington. It is thanks to them that Barilko, and so many of the people associated with his story, can still speak from the grave.

All quotes in the present tense came from the author's own in-person interviews.

A couple of quotes from Howie Meeker came from transcripts and tapes that Ted Barris provided from his research for his book *Playing Overtime: A Celebration of Oldtimers' Hockey*.

Several quotes were also taken from four videos: Oliver Solaro's *Blue Line*, TSN's feature *The Mission*, TVO's "Cross-Canada Hockey Adventures" from *The Agenda with Steve Paikin*, and Melbar Entertainment Group's *Frozen in Time: The Bill Barilko Story*.

Major Fred Paradie of the Royal Canadian Air Force History and Heritage Office provided important information about Operation Hudson. Curator Chris Johnstone of the Ontario Provincial Police Museum clarified OPP protocol of the time pertaining to the disappeared files from its investigation into the crash. Also used were the Department of Transport, Air Services, Accident Report #306 re: CF-FXT; Ted Hall's Log of Search for Aircraft C.F.-FXT, June of 1962; Ray Paterick's account of the events from May 31 to June 6, 1962; and a letter from the publisher of the *Cochrane Northland Post* dated November 22, 1962. David Black provided valuable mechanical information on Henry Hudson's Fairchild and several of his flights with Archie Chenier.

NHL.com and Hockey Reference were used for hockey statistics.

Lyrics for the "The Bill Barilko Song" ©1995 Chuck Angus SOCAN.

The following books were used for reference: Foster Hewitt's *Foster Hewitt: His Own Story*; Stan Fischler's *Power Play! The Story of the Toronto Maple Leafs*; Conn Smythe and Scott Young's *Conn Smythe: If You Can't Beat 'Em in the Alley*; Larry Milberry's *Austin Airways: Canada's Oldest Airline*; John Melady's *Overtime, Overdue: The Bill Barilko Story*; Jack Batten's *The Leafs: An Anecdotal History of the Toronto Maple Leafs*; Charlie Angus and Louie Palu's *Mirrors of Stone: Fragments from the Porcupine Frontier*; Kevin Shea's *Barilko:*

Without a Trace; Charles Wilkins' *High on the Big Stone Heart: And Further Adventures in the Boreal Heartland*; Shirlee Smith Matheson's *Lost: Unsolved Mysteries of Canadian Aviation*; Richard Buell's *The Quest: Sixteen Souls, One Magnificent Mission*; David McNeil's *In the Pressure of the Moment: Remembering Gerry McNeil*; Eric Zweig's *The Toronto Maple Leafs: The Complete Oral History*; John G. Robertson and Carl T. Madden's *Five Overtimes: The Habs and the Leafs in the 1951 Stanley Cup Finals*; and The Tragically Hip's *This Is Our Life*.

Acknowledgments

My name may be on this book, but it took an entire team to make it.

Everyone with Sutherland House Books: Ken Whyte, for proposing the book to me. Ian Coutts, foremost for caring about the book but also for seeing what I was missing and fixing what I couldn't find. Lena Yang, for the beautiful book cover. Shalomi Ranasinghe and Leah Ciani, for shepherding the book from draft to press under compressed deadlines and complex conditions. Sarah Miniaci, for bringing it out into the world, where the story needed to be heard again.

John Lister, Bill Hunter, Gaetan "Gate" Lepine, Mark Fera, Kevin Vincent, Mike Mulryan, Wayne Bozzer, Oliver "Brokentooth" Solaro, "Back Roads Bill" Steer, Darryl Deller, and Charlie Angus: Thank you for sharing and entrusting me with your stories in one form or another and at one time or another.

John Melady and Kevin Shea: Your definitive biographies of Barilko inspired me to chart my own path through the story. May another come along soon to continue to carry the story forward.

Scott Bell: For telling and showing me the truth about the fate of your screenplay. May it come to light one day and make it to film.

Frank Klisanich: I hope I've done right by your uncle's remarkable story.

Steve Paikin: My brother in the Barilko story. From that little aha moment on the set of your show, we made sure he finally got his due.

Barry Avrich, Mark Selby, Melissa Coghlan, Ken Ng, Chris Monette, Stephen Dranitsaris, Asock Kandiah, Brett Hughes, Alex Morrison, Raluca Alexe, Or Azulay, and Jonathan Karni with Melbar Entertainment Group: Thank you for bringing the Barilko story to the big screen.

Agnico Eagle, Jim Temerty, "The Onion Man," Red Wilson, Ian Ihnatowycz, Barry Green, Larry Tanenbaum, and Howard Sokolowski: You stepped up when others wouldn't and believed in the documentary with your wallets when those who should've didn't.

Chad Calaiezzi at Expedition Helicopters: Thank you for twice guiding me into the crash site. It was a moving experience both times. I promise never to ask you to do it again.

Craig Campbell, Mike Ferriman, Debbie Morin, and Jennifer Thom: I'm grateful for your assistance in helping me research the book.

Ted Barris: Thank you for quietly mentoring a fellow author.

Dr. David Armstrong, Victoria Pikor, Jedid-Jah Blom, Amanda McCaffrey, and the entire team at McMaster University Health Sciences: Without all of you, I never would've been well enough to see this book through to the end.

Dennis and Jacqueline at S&D Automotive: An honest and professional mechanic is a rare find. Thank you for keeping my ride on the road and well within budget.

My father, Ronald Shuker, in the great beyond with Barilko: I carry your name proudly. If only you could see me now.

My mother, Jill Shuker: You've always been there, no matter what. That will always be enough. Stick around for a while longer.

And K, still the GWOAT: In searching for the light through two years of darkness, I found it every day, right by my side. Everything I do is to impress you.